Quiet Escapes

First published in Great Britain in 2022 by
Greenfinch
An imprint of Quercus Editions Ltd
Carmelite House
50 Victoria Embankment
London EC4Y 0DZ

An Hachette UK company

A CIP catalogue record for this book is available
from the British Library

HB ISBN 978-1-52942-055-5
eBook ISBN: 978-1-52942-054-8

10 9 8 7 6 5 4 3 2 1

Design by Ginny Zeal
Printed and bound in Italy by L.E.G.O SpA

Quiet Escapes

50 inspiring destinations
to find your Zen

Emma Thomson

greenfinch

Contents

FOREWORD

It is early morning and I have walked into the woods behind my house in Kent in the south of England. With each step, the roar of the busy road fades until just the song of small, hidden birds, warbling in the air, envelops me. I stand stock-still and listen. Beneath my boots, the root-riddled dirt is pockmarked with the delicate footprints of deer, and high above my head stretch sweet chestnut trees, their tender young bodies swaying in the crisp wind and emitting a soft groan, as if protesting against the sun for waking them so early. It is not the most exotic scene, but it is my own perfect pocket of quiet.

The lockdowns enforced to contain the spread of Covid-19 plunged all of us into unprecedented periods of confinement. For some, this brought their first experience of prolonged quiet; for others it was a stressful, and at times claustrophobic, collision of work and home-schooling. As a result, some may say: 'Don't speak to me of quiet: I want chatter, clamour and sweet cacophony', while others may long for it. Regardless, all of us now feel our weary souls have been stretched thin. For those that cherished the quietness of lockdown and want to extend it, this book is for you. For those, exhausted and wrung out by stress, this book is for you. It is a vaccine against noise.

During my career as a travel journalist, I have always been drawn to, or sought out, the world's quieter corners and experiences. But, unable to travel, I spent the year exploring silence as if it were a new continent. I discovered it is a mysterious, practically untouched, place where few of us have travelled because, let's face it, even when we are confined, sounds and screens are never far away. How much energy do we expend staving off the incessant hum, thrum and clatter of modern life? And, in doing so, how much of ourselves also gets lost in the blocking?

Quiet Escapes is a collection of the best places I have encountered for quiet and the discreet magic it offers. It is a pilgrim's guide of sorts: I can show you the way, but the journey is yours. Quiet is making a comeback. Welcome to the silent revolution.

Emma

HOW TO TRAVEL

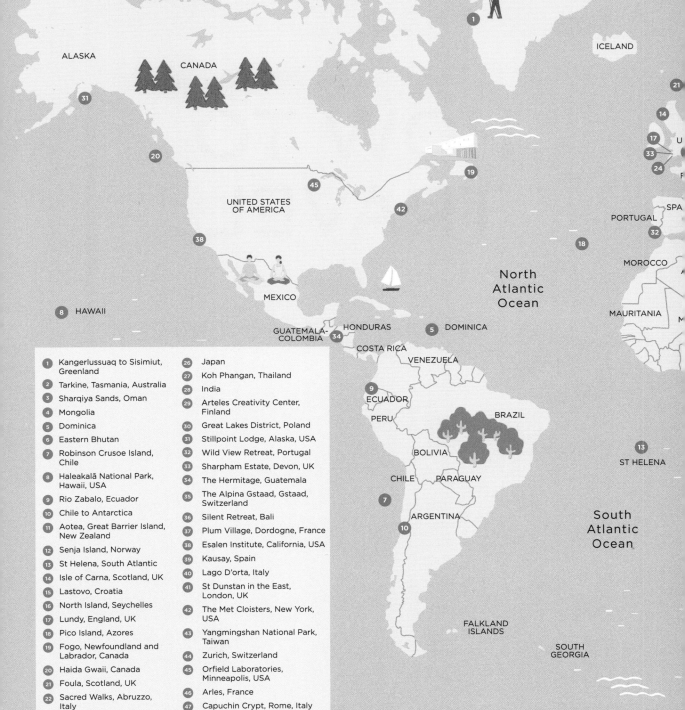

1 Kangerlussuaq to Sisimiut, Greenland
2 Tarkine, Tasmania, Australia
3 Sharqiya Sands, Oman
4 Mongolia
5 Dominica
6 Eastern Bhutan
7 Robinson Crusoe Island, Chile
8 Haleakalā National Park, Hawaii, USA
9 Rio Zabalo, Ecuador
10 Chile to Antarctica
11 Aotea, Great Barrier Island, New Zealand
12 Senja Island, Norway
13 St Helena, South Atlantic
14 Isle of Carna, Scotland, UK
15 Lastovo, Croatia
16 North Island, Seychelles
17 Lundy, England, UK
18 Pico Island, Azores
19 Fogo, Newfoundland and Labrador, Canada
20 Haida Gwaii, Canada
21 Foula, Scotland, UK
22 Sacred Walks, Abruzzo, Italy
23 Kakadu National Park, Australia
24 Dartmoor, England, UK
25 South Luangwa National Park, Zambia

26 Japan
27 Koh Phangan, Thailand
28 India
29 Arteles Creativity Center, Finland
30 Great Lakes District, Poland
31 Stillpoint Lodge, Alaska, USA
32 Wild View Retreat, Portugal
33 Sharpham Estate, Devon, UK
34 The Hermitage, Guatemala
35 The Alpina Gstaad, Gstaad, Switzerland
36 Silent Retreat, Bali
37 Plum Village, Dordogne, France
38 Esalen Institute, California, USA
39 Kausay, Spain
40 Lago D'orta, Italy
41 St Dunstan in the East, London, UK
42 The Met Cloisters, New York, USA
43 Yangmingshan National Park, Taiwan
44 Zurich, Switzerland
45 Orfield Laboratories, Minneapolis, USA
46 Arles, France
47 Capuchin Crypt, Rome, Italy
48 In Flanders Fields Museum, Ypres, Belgium
49 Leipzig, Germany
50 Yazd, Iran

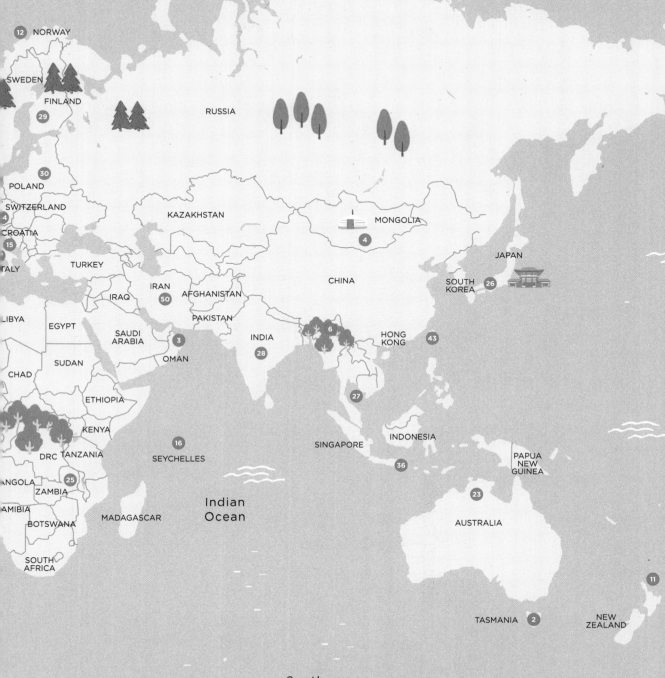

INTRODUCTION

There is a certain irony in writing about quiet. Words create boundaries around an experience that is, ultimately, vast and indescribable. For q.u.i.e.t is the space between. It is the full stop. The pause between breaths. The gap between musical notes. It is not nothing, but rather everything. It is where all meaning resides.

And, yet, enjoying quiet is a rare adventure for most of us. Our ears are bombarded daily by a seemingly ever-increasing shrill, discordant symphony of ringing telephones, pinging text message and email alerts, honking car horns, rumbling airplanes, barking dogs, and the ceaseless chatter of others all around us. Our brains are a-buzz, and we are hooked on it; driven by the dopamine rush of anticipation, while simultaneously battling the anxiety this constant noise brings.

Two-thirds of the world's population own a mobile phone and it is estimated that the average UK citizen spends three and a half hours a day on it; in the USA that rises to five hours. Our addiction is so pervasive they even have a name for it: nomophobia, the fear of not having your phone with you. It is giving us shorter attention spans and we are all getting deafer as we crank up the volume louder and louder just to be able to hear above the din. In this hyper-connected world, we need to pause and notice if we are shifting from, 'being free people to becoming resources', writes Norwegian explorer, Erling Kagge. 'We learn to live with it because we think we must, but noise is and remains a disturbing element that reduces our quality of life,' he continues.

Many of us are longing to press the off button. 'To return to something basic, authentic, to find peace, and to experience a small quiet alternative,' finishes Kagge. And still, the idea of being quiet can often be seen as boring, uncomfortable, even scary. John Cage, in his avant-garde *Lecture on Nothing,* urges us to look past this: 'We need not fear these silences, we may love them…for we are like an empty glass into which, at any moment, anything may be poured.'

And it seems that life does *will* us toward silence. All animals can hear, but not all can see, which is a clear indication we have to listen to survive. The practice of silence (in the form of prayer or meditation) is also a common denominator among all religions and spiritual practices, despite them being separated by thousands of years and miles. Artists from Mark Rothko to Claude Monet and musicians and composers such as Miles Davis and Claude Debussy, even the deaf Ludwig van Beethoven, have all harnessed silence in their work to communicate its capacity to expand our minds and thoughts.

*Paddleboarder on the mirror-calm Hobda
River in Ulgii, Western Mongolia.*

Furthermore, according to the research of professor Nina Kraus, if you take children regularly to quiet places where they can listen to nature (which the ears were made for) their neural networking will be much stronger and they will have far superior abilities to learn language and solve problems.

Quiet is the great overlooked panacea. Benefits include lower blood pressure, lower cortisol (the stress hormone) levels, easing of insomnia and improved concentration, to name a few. Some argue that silence is the new luxury; a therapy only the wealthy can afford. After all, it is money that buys homes in less-crowded neighbourhoods, with quieter spaces; it is money that purchases travel to far-flung peaceful destinations. But while silence is certainly precious, this book of 50 personally picked suggestions on where to find it will show that quiet can be found in locations both near and far and to suit a range of budgets.

And while quiet can technically be accessed anywhere, anytime, you often need to get away from your routine to go deeper into yourself, and travel to new places can help with this. Even the religious greats had to journey to find quiet and meaning; Jesus walked into the Judaean Desert for 40 days and nights; Buddha wandered through Nepal and India.

However, experiencing the benefit of quiet is not just achievable by monks and holy men; it is achievable by all. And the quickest way to access it is by paying attention to place. Places often have something to say and, frequently, to teach us. Don't allow the temptation to share the adventure verbally with a travelling companion or capture it on camera lest you miss its subtle messages. At times a place will sing, on other occasions it will whisper. Let us retrain our ears to listen to the sounds they were crafted to enjoy. For in the words of author Jay Griffiths, who spent seven years exploring the Earth's wild places: 'We were not born for pavements and escalators, but for thunder and mud.' Experiencing deep silence is a state as graceful as a hand dipped into the current of a stream; you cannot know or feel it without testing the waters. Nature is the stage. All you have to do is stand there, let it soak into your bones and feel your soul unclench.

The soft folds of the Sharqiya Sands desert in Oman.

Seeking Quiet in a Noisy World

Quiet is the new cool. Forward-thinking businesses are creating quiet zones, meditation/nap rooms, Zen rooftop gardens and installing pods – convertible lounge chairs with hoods that can be pulled down for privacy. Hotels, supermarkets and even airports are also waking up to the benefits of creating peaceful spaces. At the time of writing, there are 17 airports worldwide that have gone silent (i.e. all announcements are banned in the main waiting area) including Dubai Airport, Delhi's Indira Gandhi International Airport and Singapore Changi Airport. The concept of pop-up silent cafés is growing, and every year in April there is a global Noise Awareness Day.

Quiet is sparking social movements, such as the collaboration between Mimi (a German hearing technology company) and the Good Hearing Initiative who launched a nationwide campaign in 2020 called #silenceforfuture to make people stop and think about the level of noise they are living with day-to-day and have them talk about it. And, 'the latest trend in luxury travel doesn't involve thread count or a seaweed-mud wrap. It's quiet. Hotels from luxury resorts to business-travel chains are marketing things like noise-free zones, triple-paned glass, soundproof walls, and serene settings where the whole sell is the ability to hear a pin drop,' reports Leigh Gallagher in Fortune.com.

For the first time in history, rather than just trying to reduce noise levels generally, our quiet areas – from tracts of wilderness and urban parks to city idylls and marine parks – are being actively protected via the Quiet Parks International initiative (see page 19). These will become beacons for travellers seeking quiet.

All this shows that quiet while travelling is not unattainable. It just sometimes requires a little bit more awareness and effort. Some of the places suggested in this book may take longer to get to, but the payoff for peace is priceless.

Being a Quiet Traveller

Going on a quiet trip plays a part in the growing movement of travelling with purpose; a trend that was encouraged before, but in light of pressing concerns about climate change, should really be the norm. Quiet travellers consciously aim to be slower, greener and more sustainable in their choice of destination.

This could involve taking fewer trips and staying for longer to reduce our environmental impact; being aware of how much noise we are generating on location (see page 17 for tips on how to reduce this); and perhaps choosing to support local accommodation providers instead of staying in big-brand chain hotels that leave large carbon footprints. It could mean exploring on foot or by bike while in situ instead of choosing noise-polluting taxis, buses and trains, or swapping visits to well-known Instagrammed-to-death sites for lesser-known spots that perhaps give you a glimpse of the city or country's truer character. Travelling to quieter locations also eases the pressure of over-tourism on iconic routes such as Iceland's Golden Circle, regions like southern Bali and Thailand, or bucket-list sites such as Machu Picchu in Peru. In turn, this benefits local communities by spreading revenue more evenly.

Quiet travellers are not passive, they are present. They put down their cameras and drones and look; they sit and listen to the stories of locals, instead of staying within the comfort of a group; and they let the landscape speak.

SEVEN WAYS TO TRAVEL MORE PEACEFULLY

Setting off

Build in peace as soon as you leave the front door by factoring in extra time, so you do not have to rush. Book a seat at the front of the plane away from the engines located under the wings; you could even go as far as selecting an aisle seat; they are four decibels quieter than window seats, which are closer to the skin of the aircraft.

Do not overplan

When visiting a new place, the temptation to see as much as possible can be strong. Try to resist overplanning. Leave entire days empty and just let the time unfold – see what comes, whether it is lingering in a café for an hour or two to observe life playing out in front of you, or sitting in a field listening to the wind and noticing the to-ing and fro-ing of minute insects.

Switch off

For many of us, the reliance on electronics is strong and their constant use ingrained. Try leaving your phone, smartwatch or tablet in the hotel – not just switching them off – and remember what life felt like before we ever had them. Look up and listen to the place you are in.

Pack earplugs

There are some parts of travelling that are inherently noisy – airports, public transport, etc. Invest in some good-quality foam earplugs and muffle it all out.

Timing is everything

It cannot be avoided: even some of the world's quietest places at times suffer from busy periods. Arrange to travel during low season and if you are visiting a well-known site, such as a national park, try to visit early in the day or last thing in the evening to have the best chance of enjoying longer stretches of silence.

Be mindful

Quiet travellers leave no trace. They take their rubbish with them; they do not yell or shout if they are trying to get someone's attention; and they do not use drones for photography. They tread softly and respectfully.

Learn to listen

It is often said that we are not really paying attention to someone during a conversation, if we are already thinking about how we will respond while they are still talking. The same applies when responding to life. True listening requires focus and presence and, much like an onion, sounds are layered. The longer you stay still, the more these layers will slowly be revealed to you as your ears adjust to the new soundscape.

QUIET PARKS INTERNATIONAL

Ask most people to reel off a list of things that are at risk of extinction and they will quote tigers, pandas or the polar ice caps. But quietness – never. Turns out we should be concerned.

'Noise is blanketing the planet and natural quiet has become an endangered species without people knowing it,' according to Emmy-winning acoustic ecologist, Gordon Hempton.

'Most people on Earth, 55 per cent, live in urban areas (this will rise to 68 per cent by 2041) and refrigerators, air-conditioning systems and airplanes are a few of the things that have become part of the ambient sound that prevents us from listening to the natural sounds of our environment. But it is our birthright to listen, quietly and undisturbed, to the natural environment and take whatever meanings we may from it,' says Hempton.

He goes on to say that, 'Science has made it abundantly clear that noise pollution is not just an annoyance, it causes health loss,' and shockingly, it is estimated that nine out of ten children alive today will never experience quiet in their lives unless things change. Yet, as recently as 2018, no-one was protecting it.

Hempton grew up amid quiet. His father was stationed at Pearl Harbour, outside of Honolulu, prior to the arrival of tourism in Hawaii. 'The jungle was my backyard; my best friends were all insects,' says Hempton, but his first memory of silence was at the bottom of the community swimming pool. 'I would let my air out and sink to the bottom and feel swaddled by the pressure of the water.'

But the experience that would shape the direction of his entire life did not come until much later. 'One day, after enrolling in graduate school, a thunderstorm rolled over me – and for the first time I really heard it. I lay on the ground and listened and felt alive.' In the four decades since, he has circled the globe three times in pursuit of and recording Earth's rarest natural sounds.

His first attempt to protect these sounds was the One Square Inch of Silence project – a small red stone symbolically placed in Hoh Rainforest at Olympic National Park, near his home in Seattle, with a view to it becoming the world's first quiet park. Forming the largest swathe of virgin temperate rainforest in the western hemisphere, 'it was once the least noise-polluted place in the United States, until the US Navy decided that this little-used airspace would become an electronic-warfare exercise range and fly over it thousands of times in the world's noisiest jets,' explains Hempton.

Hoh Rainforest at Olympic National Park, Washington State, USA – the world's first Quiet Park.

For 13 years, Hempton campaigned to protect it, but with no luck. And then the stone that marked the one square inch was taken. 'So on a day when the US Navy weren't flying, I went into the forest and asked the Quiet what I had done wrong and where I went from here. And the Quiet answered! It laughed at me and said, "It's just a rock. Isn't there another one?"' And on that day in 2018, Hempton co-founded Quiet Parks International (QPI) – the world's only non-profit organization committed to saving quiet (rather than just reducing noise). Until its formation, not a single location on planet Earth was off limits to noise pollution.

So what counts as noise? 'Noise pollution is any loud simple-information sound that denies us access to the faint, often complex, and survival-relevant sounds that provide meaning to our lives,' explains Hempton. He and the QPI team aim to protect six key areas: Wilderness Quiet Parks, Urban Quiet Parks, Quiet Trails, Marine Quiet Parks, Quiet Residences and Communities, and Quiet Stays.

To determine if they qualify, QPI sound recordists measure and look for the noise-free intervals in an average morning between two hours prior to sunrise until one hour after sunrise. (These parameters change for marine parks because sound travels many times faster and more clearly through water than through air.) 'Anything over 15 minutes without a human-caused noise intrusion is considered world class. To a layperson this may seem easy to achieve, but it's not – despite what peaceful photographs of the national parks suggest,' says Hempton.

In fact, it is so unusual that only 12 or 13 sites have been identified across the entire USA (excluding Hawaii and Alaska). At the time of writing, there is currently one certified Wilderness Quiet Park (see page 61), with nine pending; and four Urban Quiet Parks (see pages 213 and 215), with another six awaiting certification. 'By recognizing and awarding tranquil areas and inviting people to listen to the outer quiet, we help them to find the source of silence within themselves,' says Hempton. 'All those nagging questions in our modern lives seem unanswerable because you need to find your way home and ask those questions there (see box, page 21). And your home is a quiet place. Don't listen *for* something; just notice how a place makes you feel.'

However, preserving quiet is not just for our peace of mind. 'Quiet places are inherently healthy places,' says Hempton. It seems our ears are attuned to sounds that help us not just to survive but thrive. 'Humans have an incredible hearing range – from 20 to 20,000 vibrations per second – that allows us to interpret tremendous beauty in life, such as the wind passing through trees and the rhythm of crashing surf – none of which is of much survival relevance to us. And yet...our peak sensitivity falls within range of 2.5 kilohertz. And do you know what other sound corresponds perfectly to this? Not other human voices, but birdsong. Birdsong is the number one indicator of habitats prosperous to humans. If birds are singing, there's food, water and enough resources to raise young,' explains Hempton.

So when we ask ourselves why something we cannot see, touch, taste or hear needs our protection, Hempton says: 'Because when we save quiet, we save the Earth – we save the places that produce clean air, we keep biodiversity and we protect endangered species. When you enter a church there are no signs saying, 'Be Quiet'; it is implicit. There is an accepted code of behaviour. It is the same with Quiet Parks: if people know it is a designated quiet area, they will explore with a different code of behaviour.'

You can learn more and support the work of QPI at quietparks.org

(Opposite) The peaceful meander of Lutownia River, a tributary of the Narewka River in Bialowieza Forest, Poland.

ASKING QUESTIONS OF THE QUIET

It may be an oxymoron but asking questions to the Quiet can yield answers that do not otherwise easily reveal themselves. When you are in a quiet place it takes time for stillness to descend, for the lake to become calm, the wind to stop blowing, but eventually stillness will settle upon you. When it does, pull out a list of questions that you have been unable to solve – they can be about business, family, etc. – and ask the Quiet out loud. The first emotion you feel is the answer – hang onto it and gently tease it apart. The most common answer is usually: 'That's not important.'

Gordon Hempton, co-founder Quiet Parks International

INTO THE WILDERNESS

'And into the forest I go, to lose my mind and find my soul.'

JOHN MUIR

How to do it: Greenland
is an autonomous
territory of Denmark,
so Air Greenland
flights depart from
Copenhagen direct to
Kangerlussuaq. On
completing the trek,
most travellers take an
internal flight from
Sisimiut back to
Kangerlussuaq. Visas
aren't required. This isn't
a technical trail, but it
requires preparation.
Provisions cannot be
obtained en route and
should be purchased
from the Pilersuisoq
supermarket in
Kangerlussuaq, or
Pisiffik in Sisimiut. There
are unstaffed wooden
huts dotted along the
trail furnished only with
bunk beds and no other
facilities. They can't be
pre-booked, so most
trekkers prefer to carry
and pitch their own tent.
Hostels and hotels are
available in both
Kangerlussuaq and
Sisimiut.

Best time of year: The
trail is open only from
mid-June to mid-
September but be
aware mosquitoes can
hatch in full force at the
start of the season –
bring a headnet. Also
pack an eye mask to
block out the midnight
sun and aid sleep.

Hike Greenland's remote Arctic Circle Trail

KANGERLUSSUAQ TO SISIMIUT, GREENLAND

Travel to the top of the world and spend ten days inside the Arctic Circle, yet outside of time

Picture a place of soft polar silence, where whales slink through the shallows and 15,000-year-old icebergs waltz slowly in the bay. A timeless kind of quiet that you can feel in your bones. A rich nothingness made for the mind, not the ears. Few of us know what to do with it anymore, but Greenland can remind you.

Locals call their homeland Kalaalit Nunnat, meaning 'Land of the People', which is ironic given that it is the least densely populated territory on Earth – home to just 56,565 people in an area roughly half the size of Europe. Out here, nature is King. Eighty per cent of the island is crowned by a vast ancient ice cap, dogs outnumber people two to one and, come winter, the sun packs up and heads south for two and a half months, leaving the land with the lights off. There are just 13 main towns and no roads or railways running between them. The only way of getting around is via helicopter, boat...or foot.

And here is Greenland's 'sole' secret: it isn't entirely frozen like the Arctic or Antarctic. Come summer, the fringes of the world's largest island are, in fact, green. A verdant wash of wildflower-covered tundra brimming with blueberries, crowberries and mushrooms – terrain ripe for off-the-beaten-track hiking.

The Arctic Circle Trail is a backcountry route that stretches for 160km (100 miles) from Kangerlussuaq, on the edge of the vast interior ice sheet, to Sisimiut, Greenland's second-largest town, on the shores of the Labrador Sea. There are simple russet-coloured huts – some no larger than garden sheds – dotted along the trail, but most hikers prefer to wild camp so they can fully embrace the trail's gift of silence and the opportunity it provides to disconnect. Because outside of the two towns there is no mobile phone signal and, on average, only 300 hikers a year attempt the route, so it's possible to go days without seeing or hearing from another soul.

One of the peaceful cottages at Glacier Lodge Eqi, Illulissat, Greenland.

Jordan Trail, Jordan: In Biblical times, there was an ancient trade route that stretched from Egypt to Syria known as the King's Highway. Some say Jesus walked along it. This 644-km (400-mile) long trail, that runs from Umm Qais, in the north, to Aqaba on the Red Sea, traces a section of it and, rather appropriately given the links to Jesus, it takes 40 days to complete.

Transcaucasian Trail, Georgia and Armenia: Still under development, this long-distance trail, best undertaken between May and September, connects more than 20 national parks and a host of UNESCO-listed sites that have earned it the moniker of the 'New Silk Road'. Expect alpine meadows, glacial rivers and 1,000-year-old churches.

Damodar Saribung Traverse, Nepal: If you've always wanted to get a glimpse of Tibetan culture, this trek, which is counted as one of Nepal's most-remote trails and rarely attempted by westerners, will lead you to it. Best for experienced trekkers because it can tip into mountaineering when crossing the 6,042-m (19,822-ft) high Saribung Pass.

Pitch your tent on the Greenland ice cap and listen to its songs.

Explore the great big silence of Greenland.

It will just be you and the whispering wind, as you traverse mossy tundra beneath massive skies, ford glacial rivers and wade through fields of pom-pom cotton grass, past mirror-calm lakes, stone cairns knighted by bleached reindeer antlers and small sandy sweeps of beach. Your only visitors will be the occasional snow-white Arctic hare, grazing reindeer, shy amber-eyed Arctic foxes and the world's fastest bird, the peregrine falcon, with its high-pitched cry.

Days are stripped of fast-paced decision making and instead blissfully simplified into breaking camp, walking and building camp. And what's more, the trail is only open in summer, so you'll experience near constant daylight. Breathe it all in. Indeed, freedom is such a natural part of life here that the Greenlanders don't even have a word for it. It should also be added, your hiking bears purpose. International mining companies are moving in to excavate the island's rich deposits of uranium, iron and platinum, but supporting tourism can help provide Greenlanders with a more sustainable future.

Explore an ancient rainforest

THE LOWDOWN

How to do it: The international gateway to Tasmania is Hobart International Airport. From there, take an internal flight to Burnie/ Wynyard Airport and hire a rental car (all the main companies have offices at the airport) and drive 50 minutes to Smithton, the main gateway to the region. The Tarkine is remote, so load your car with supplies and keep a note of where fuel stations are located.

Best time of year: Tasmania has a temperate climate meaning summers are mild and winters not overly cold. However, the Tarkine is the wettest area receiving on average 2,400mm (94.5in) of rainfall annually.

TARKINE, TASMANIA, AUSTRALIA

Tasmania's wilderness offers a glimpse of a world that has hardly changed since dinosaurs roamed the Earth

Nestled in the far northwest of Tasmania, Tarkine is Australia's largest tract of Gondwanan rainforest – a 180-million-year-old lost world filled with plant species that have been around since the island was connected to New Zealand, Papua New Guinea and Patagonia. Here, amid forests of tree ferns as tall as parasols, you could be the only person for miles. Pronounced 'tar-kine' to rhyme with 'fine', not 'mean', this forgotten landscape is not named on maps, but roughly falls within the area between Arthur River to the north, Pieman River to the south and the Murchison Highway to the east. It is a National Heritage site comprised of a jumble of myrtle, leatherwood and pine, clad in verdant mosses, lichens and liverworts; quivering plains of button grass; and rivers, caves and sandy beaches combed by wind-whipped waves. The habitats harbour many species of rare or endangered wildlife, such as the orange-bellied parrot and the only surviving wild population of Tasmanian devil. It is even whispered that Tasmanian tigers still stalk the Tarkine region: it was officially declared extinct in 1936 and yet this striped carnivorous marsupial, with an abdominal pouch like that of a kangaroo, is often the subject of (unproven) sightings.

The territory is also of great spiritual importance. It is named after the Tarkiner people, an Aboriginal tribe which hunted and dreamed on this coastline for 30,000 years. They left one of the greatest caches of Aboriginal sites in Australia, including the remains of beehive-shaped bark huts, stone-tool quarries and shell middens of foraged oysters and mussels. These are concentrated and conserved in areas such as West Point Reserve and the Arthur-Pieman Conservation Area to revive Tasmanian Aboriginal culture that was oppressed, enslaved and discriminated against to the point of eradication by colonial English invaders.

Tours via helicopter, river, 4WD or on foot are offered, but most travellers choose to follow the Tarkine Drive, a well signposted 205-km (127-mile) self-drive loop which begins and ends in the town of Smithton. Highlights en route include: the 'Edge of

The raw beauty of Philosopher Falls in Tasmania's Tarkine wilderness.

the World' lookout across a Pacific wave-battered bluff; the fishing-shack settlement of Couta Rocks; Sumac lookout over Arthur River; the mirror-still Lake Chisholm where you can occasionally spot platypus; and the green (not strawberry pink) Milkshake Hills.

Sites worth making a detour for are: Dip Falls, a most unusual waterfall that tumbles over an amphitheatre of hexagonal basalt columns; the nearby Big Tree, a eucalyptus some 17m (56ft) wide; the 'surf city' of Marrawah; and the colonial town of Stanley, which is squeezed between the curves of two sandy beaches and overshadowed by the looming mass of The Nut, a sheer-sided solidified volcanic lava lake that you can hike up (or catch the chairlift) for sweeping views of the Tarkine. Keep an eye out for the fairy penguins huddled along Godfrey's Beach north of town.

Some areas of the region are conserved, but mining of gold, tin and osmiridium, as well as logging, threaten those unprotected parts. Conservationists are working hard to safeguard the territory, and travellers can help change happen by visiting.

Tarkine offers an off-grid experience through a rare habitat with immersion in otherworldly and ancient rainforests and the chance to see species found nowhere else on Earth – maybe even the long-believed-extinct Tasmanian tiger.

Dawn reflections on the Pieman River in the Tarkine Wilderness, Tasmania, Australia.

ALSO TRY

Christmas Island, Australia: So-called because it was discovered on Christmas Day in 1643, this Australian territory is famous for its annual red crab migration between November and December when 100 million of the crustaceans form a moving carpet toward the ocean to spawn. Not to mention all manner of birds.

Norfolk Island, Australia: Some 1,456km (905 miles) off the coast of Byron Bay, this island of rolling green hills that mingle with pine-tree-framed sandy bays is largely a designated national park. Fascinatingly, it is also where Australia's worst convicts were sent during the colony's early days and those penal settlements are now World Heritage sites.

Heard and McDonald Islands, Australia: Closer to Antarctica than Australia, this ice-covered pair have, to date, only been visited by 240 people and to get there you will need to join an expedition. They are UNESCO-listed thanks to having one of the last pristine ecosystems on Earth – with zero introduced species.

Experience the acetic charm of the desert

SHARQIYA SANDS, OMAN

THE LOWDOWN

How to do it: Muscat is the nearest international airport. Most travellers must purchase an e-visa prior to travel. Oman Air services routes from most major cities worldwide. Trips into the desert should be organized with a reputable tour operator.

Best time of year: Summers (June–August) in Oman are sweltering; the best time to visit is between October and April when the mercury stays below 35°C (95°F).

'The desert is a natural extension of the inner silence of the body.'
Jean Baudrillard

Of the Earth's four main landscapes – mountains, jungle, sea and desert – only the last offers a vacuum of quiet heat that can defrost the soul and strip life back to the brain-calming basics of water and walking. A monastic, seemingly barren environment that has inspired many, such as the famous Desert Fathers, to connect with something higher.

Because out here, where you're robbed of larger-than-life visual and auditory distractions, there's space to focus on the minutiae, such as the s-shaped squiggle of a snake trail or a beetle gathering beads of morning dew.

There are lessons to be learned amid a landscape that's redesigned anew each day, as the wind makes the dunes walk. Lessons on how to live without need and how to appreciate the fundamentals of life, such as water; lessons in letting go when you're at the mercy of the elemental sandstorms or scorching heat. It's an atmosphere that peels away the ego and, rather than getting lost, this is a wilderness that reveals the true you because there is literally nothing to hide behind – not a single rock.

Celebrity deserts such as the Sahara are well visited (not to mention large swathes of it are currently earmarked as unsafe), so consider instead an underdog option: Oman's Sharqiya Sands. Formerly known as the Wahiba Desert, its bosomy dunes stretch for 160km (100 miles) across the eastern quarter of Oman that bulges into the Arabian Sea and, unlike its strict Islamic neighbours, Saudi Arabia and Yemen, Oman is a safe sultanate often nicknamed the 'Switzerland of the Middle East'.

The landscape is home to the Bedouin, nomadic Arab tribes who still lead their camels across the shifting terrain and run a few simple tented camps in a country relatively new to tourism.

Experience the quiet of the Omani desert from the back of a camel.

ALSO TRY

Namib Desert, Namibia: In places the oxidised orange sands of the Namib-Naukluft National Park in western Namibia rise 300m (980ft) above sea level, making them the tallest dunes in the world. Be sure to hike the sandy hills surrounding the famous Sossusvlei clay pan at dawn and see the 700-year-old preserved trees here.

Gobi Desert, China, Mongolia: Spread between north-eastern China and the southern Mongolian steppe, the Gobi is steeped in Silk Road history and is bejewelled with fossil treasures and home to the endangered double-humped Bactrian camel. It is also home to remains of the Great Wall of China.

Atacama Desert, Chile: Curled around the Pacific coastline in Chile's northern region, the driest desert in the world – often compared to the planet Mars – is famous for its eyeball-blazing white salt lakes visited by Andean flamingos and vast sand dunes visited by the chinchilla-like viscacha.

Rise in the lilac haze before dawn, ascend a high dune, sit on its soft rim – curved as a spine – and watch the sun's rays, splayed like fingers, paint the clouds peach, orange and amber as they pierce the horizon. Afterwards, you can return to camp for breakfast, nibbling candy-sweet dates and learning to cook fresh *gursh* (Bedouin flatbread) over smouldering campfire embers.

The real magic, however, intensifies as the day departs. The rich light turns the warm sand into wrinkled silk around your footprints. Goats, nibbling in vain at the sparse grasses, herd themselves towards the camp corral; and the camels – their old-men grumbles reverberating across the sand – become silhouetted on the horizon. After an open-air shower beneath the rising moon, you're drawn towards the honeyed lilt of Arabic voices coming from a central campfire, where flames dance around an old metal teapot. Seated beside it is a local Bedouin, who starts caressing bittersweet melodies from a pear-shaped *oud* (lute) and you lie back on the cushions, listening to

TOP TIPS

In Oman the weekend falls on Friday and Saturday and businesses may be closed, so plan your activities accordingly. It's respectful to cover your shoulders and legs, particularly outside of the main cities.

the ancient songs. Soon another musician begins to pound his *darbuka* (drum) and the beat intensifies heralding the 'camel dance' – a two-step sand shuffle.

When the moon is high you retire to your simple tent, where a candle-lit Arabian lantern projects celestial patterns onto the canvas roof. But you prefer the real thing, so you pull the camp bed outside where stars spread across the unpolluted night, bright as spilt sugar, the smell of wood smoke in your hair.

ABOVE LEFT *Believed to be more than 1,500 years old, the elegant Nakhal Fort has been renovated many times but retains its old soul.*

ABOVE *Brewing tea over desert coals.*

Channel your inner nomad on the Mongolian steppe

MONGOLIA

THE LOWDOWN

How to do it: Chinggis Khaan International Airport is the gateway to the Mongolian steppe. Mongolia grants visa-free access to citizens of 24 countries, including the USA. All other nationalities (including UK citizens) should apply for a 30-day visa prior to travel. Ger camps range from basic to luxurious and should be booked in advance. Those wishing to wild camp can rent a 4WD campervan with a roof-top tent from a reputable provider in the capital Ulaanbaatar. Rentals from private individuals should be avoided. You can book a driver too, if required.

Best time of year: It's best to travel in summer (June–September); winters are brutally cold and plunge the mercury to -30°C (-22°F).

Experience a life without boundaries in this untrammelled wilderness

On arriving in the world's largest landlocked country, an odd feeling will plague you. It's not an acute discomfort; just a sensation that circulates in the back of your brain – a whispering or nagging you can't ignore. A few days later, it will dawn on you that the oddity is space – boundless and bountiful.

So many of us are used to a boxed-in life where skyscrapers block out the heavens, where fences or hedges corral us. But in Mongolia – the world's least-populated nation – you can roam freely across endless expanses of grassy steppe, carved up only by mountains and rushing rivers. There are no clamouring crowds, no noisy construction sites, no smog-laden roads tarring the land. Nothing bars your way as you wander across vast plains toward an ever-broadening horizon.

Half of the country's 3.3 million population lives in the (vowel-tastic) capital of Ulaanbaatar; the remainder still live a nomadic lifestyle, moving between summer and winter camps with their flocks of sheep, goats and occasional yak. Here, the horse, not the car, is the predominant means of transport.

Outside of the capital, with its angular Soviet-style buildings, it feels as if little has changed here since the times of Genghis Khan – the founder of the Mongol Empire who, in the 12th century, united the nomadic tribes under his leadership. While his military campaigns often decimated the towns and populations of his adversaries, to the people of Mongolia he was seen as a liberator who brought culture, technology and religious freedom to the Mongolian Empire.

Tibetan Buddhist monasteries surrounded by stupas stand sentinel, seemingly in the middle of nowhere, their prayer flags shivering in the lively wind. Two-humped Bactrian camels, that once served as pack animals on the Silk Road, still roam wild in parts of the country. And, everywhere, life is steeped in ritual: from blessing *ovoo* (sacred stone heaps) with *airag* (fermented mare's milk) to not stepping on the threshold when entering or exiting a ger (yurt).

The vast Hulunbuir Grasslands spread without fences across inner Mongolia.

Herding horses through Gorkhi Terelj National Park, Mongolia.

These 'white pearls of the steppe' are circular felt-lined tents with ornately painted miniature wooden doors. Ducking your head to enter reveals a central cast-iron stove; its flue protruding through the roof and its innards crackling with flames. All of family life unfolds around this fire: it provides warmth, food and, during the dark winters, light.

Anyone has the right to camp where they want to in Mongolia and intrepid travellers can enjoy unparalleled freedom wild camping, but for those who prefer a few more comforts, the Mongolian version of a hotel is a *ger* camp; a cluster of tents, usually with a separate restaurant. They not only preserve the traditional culture, but also don't leave a scar on the landscape. Interiors feature low-rise wooden beds, hand-carved furniture, layers of rugs and often wall hangings.

To fully experience a glimpse of nomad life, family-run *ger buudals* are a good bet. You can join the family milking yaks, preparing noodle soup and sharing bowls of salted tea and – if you're lucky – they might break out the *morin khuur* (a traditional fiddle) and strike up a few tunes.

Otherwise, days are spent riding, visiting natural hot springs and monasteries and, when the cold cloak of night creeps in and your eyes can't count another star, you can bed down inside your snug cocoon and settle beside the ever-lit fire. You'll be surprised how quickly you feel at home. After all, nomadic blood runs in all our veins – if we give it free rein.

ALSO TRY

Loch Lomond and The Trossachs, Scotland, UK: Scotland is the only place in the UK that allows widespread wild camping, and where better than amid the lochs, glens and braes of The Trossachs National Nature Reserve, which is often billed as the mini Highlands. Try to avoid the clouds of summertime midges.

Sal Salis, Australia: Spread along the shores of the Ningaloo Reef at the tip of Western Australia, this luxury eco-retreat melts into the dunes and has 15 safari-style tents. There's no internet or Wi-Fi, so you can really immerse yourself in the raw environment: from marvelling at the IDA Dark Sky-status nighttime sky, to snorkelling alongside the famed gentle-giant whale sharks.

Hossa National Park, Finland: Finland's newest national park is a rugged lake-dotted playground of pine and spruce, whose Sami name translates as 'a place far away'. Stay in rustic cabins or camp wild while clustered around a roaring campfire. Don't miss the Värikallio rock paintings; they're the country's oldest.

Enjoy tourist-free peace in the Caribbean

THE LOWDOWN

How to do it: Dominica has no international airport. Travellers must first fly to Antigua or Barbados and catch a connecting flight with Caribbean airline Liat; same-day connections are not always possible. Entry is visa-free for almost all nationalities. There is also an inter-island ferry that departs from neighbouring Martinique or Guadeloupe.

Best time of year: December–June are the sunniest months; July–December the wettest.

DOMINICA

Discover the wildest Caribbean island of them all

Dominica is the Caribbean's best-kept secret. Sandwiched between the French sisters of Guadeloupe and Martinique, it's a primeval playground often likened to Jurassic Park – without the dinosaurs. An ageless landscape of rainforest-clad volcanoes, hidden tumbling waterfalls, and multitudinous rivers that run into coral reefs wriggling with rainbow-hued fish.

But this is not a fly 'n' flop destination with bleach-blond beaches crowded with sun loungers (most beaches are rocky or made of volcanic sand); it's a young island still being formed, in fact. You can feel it rising to its full potential beneath your feet: from boiling crater lakes to the bubbles that effervesce between the rocks on Champagne beach, heating the sea water so it feels like a warm bath.

It is an island seemingly designed for full-pelt adrenalin-filled adventure – after all it was the filming location for the caper-filled *Pirates of the Caribbean* franchise. You can go river tubing, canyoning, kayaking, hiking, diving and snorkelling. But it's included in this book because, on this isle that time forgot, you also have the chance to revel in raw nature and go deeper. To take pleasure in the senses, by lingering over the scent of mangoes in the marketplace, stopping in the humid forest to listen to the whistles, whoops and chirrups of birds, or plunge yourself into a silent marine world beneath the waves.

First, you will need to tap into the songlines that shaped it. Claimed by the French in 1632, it became a nation of plantation owners who imported West African slaves to work the coffee fields. Today, the majority of the population are descendants of these slaves, but Dominica is also the only eastern Caribbean island to still have a community of Caribs – 3,500 Kalinago people of Amerindian descent. You can visit Kalinago Barana Autê, their cultural centre, to understand how they connect with the land.

Take a cooling dip in Dominica's Emerald Pool in the Morne Trois Pitons National Park.

As you would expect, there's a strong connection to the natural world. The island isn't nicknamed 'Nature Island of the Caribbean' for nothing! Heck, even its flag is emblazoned with an image of the endemic Sisserou parrot – just one of the 194 bird species found here that will have twitchers glued to their binoculars.

Enjoy slow explorations of the jungles of UNESCO-listed Morne Trois Pitons National Park, looking and listening for the whistling agouti (a guinea pig-like rodent), the grunt and growl of the manicou (a type of possum), the ribbit of the critically endangered 'mountain chicken' (one of the largest species of frog in the world, so-called because it was once a popular snack among locals), or spot the coils of a three-metre-long boa constrictor wrapped around a tree.

Don a scuba mask and spend time in the company of sea turtles with their Mona Lisa smiles (four of the seven species of turtle are found here), torpedo-fast spinner, pantropical and bottlenose dolphins and best of all whales – pilot, humpback and false killer – which visit these waters all year round. Sperm whales – of *Moby Dick* fame – breed and calve here and Dominica is one of only three places in the world where you can swim with them. Hovering in the outer-space-like deep blue, their massive grey bulk suspended before you, you will look into their eye, large as a hand, and see a soul that has witnessed depths we can only imagine. A look of utter peace that will echo in your own heart.

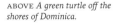

ABOVE *A green turtle off the shores of Dominica.*

RIGHT *The rocky outcrop of Glassy Point has several pools that transform into open-air swimming pools on calm days – it can be reached via an easy 2.5 km (1½mile) round trek departing from the village of Boetica.*

Montserrat, Caribbean: Eric Clapton, Elton John and Paul McCartney have all recorded albums on this quiet green isle, which is the least-visited in the Caribbean. Rebuilding is still taking place following a volcanic eruption in 1995, but 40 per cent of the island has been declared safe and the local economy needs tourism. With no large hotels or cruise terminals, it offers a slice of authentic Caribbean life.

San Blas Islands, Panama: A remote autonomous coral archipelago, home to the indigenous Guna people. Here travellers are invited as 'guests', and life is stripped of mod cons. You'll sleep in huts, dine on fish and rice and bedtime is whenever the generator runs out.

Martinique, Caribbean: The island artist Paul Gauguin called home is equally as rugged as neighbouring Dominica, with an added dash of Parisian glamour in the towns. Silence seekers should make a beeline for the peaceful beaches around Le Carbet, the wild Caravelle Peninsula and sleepy Grand Rivière.

Travel an unconquered country

EASTERN BHUTAN

THE LOWDOWN

How to do it: Wild Frontiers offers tailor-made holidays to Bhutan, including a 10-day private tour covering the Haa Valley, using a mixture of small hotels and homestays and a private guide who can translate for you when needed.

Best time to visit: Either during spring (March–May) when the valleys are a riot of rhododendrons in bloom, or in autumn (October–November) when the humidity of summer has eased. Avoid the June–September monsoon season.

Choose a country that values Gross National Happiness above Gross Domestic Product

Finding a place untrammelled by tourism is a tall order, but landlocked Bhutan is a land like no other. Hidden amid the high walls of the Himalayas, locals call this fairytale-like kingdom *Druk Yul* – Land of the Thunder Dragon – in reference to the storms that swirl through the shark-tooth-sharp mountains.

Closed to visitors until 1974 and ruled over by a succession of Dragon Kings, the country had never been colonised or conquered and so remained culturally pure until then. The first roads were only laid in the 1960s, there was no TV until 1990, there are no traffic lights, law dictates that 60 per cent of the country must always be covered in forest to keep the environment in balance and the government of Bhutan famously measures progress not by Gross Domestic Product, but by Gross National Happiness because: 'the rich are not always happy, but the happy generally consider themselves to be rich.' Little wonder it's referred to as the real-life Shangri-La.

Indeed, there's a unique sense of serenity and peace to be found here – and just a dash of quirkiness, too, thanks to the astrology readings after the national news, and ejaculating penises painted on buildings, trucks and shops to ward off evil spirits. Most travellers come to see the famous 17th-century Paro Taktsang monastery that clings to cliffs like a swallow's nest and marks the spot where Guru Rinpoche, one of the founding fathers of Tibetan Buddhism, is said to have landed on the back of a tiger and spent three years meditating in a cave. However, travel further east to the Haa Valley – which only opened up about six years ago – and you're unlikely to see another traveller.

The tiered rice fields of Punakha Valley, Bhutan.

Kyrgyzstan: The midpoint of the Silk Road, this land-locked nation of fertile plains and snow-dusted mountains has been nicknamed 'The Most Beautiful Country in the World'. Experience a life lived on horseback, where falconry, *manas* (epic poems) and music played on the *komuz* (three-stringed lute) are still popular pastimes. CBTAIay can book you into a homestay for total immersion.

Iran: This Middle-Eastern jewel, believed by many to be the cradle of civilization, is perhaps one of the world's most misjudged countries. Iranians are renowned for their above-and-beyond hospitality and Surfiran can arrange stays with local families – both nomadic and town based – so travellers can sample a home-cooked dinner and ask all those questions they might otherwise be too shy to. Check your country's travel advice before going.

Here, homestays allow hosts to earn a living without having to migrate to the larger towns in search of work and, in return, travellers get to experience real immersion in Bhutanese culture. Accommodation is often simple – a mattress on the floor and simple bathroom facilities – but the days have quiet heart. You'll sit around the wood-burning stove, sipping *chai* and frying chillies to make the favourite national dish, *ema datshi* (chillies and cheese); heat rocks to a glowing red in the fire and then plunge them, sizzling and spitting, into a wooden outdoor bathtub sprinkled with fresh herbs to bathe; sip and celebrate with *ara*, the local fermented rice wine; and possibly be dressed by your host in the traditional woven *kira* and silken *wonju* for woman, or a *gho* for men.

You can explore, at leisure, local monasteries with gilded statues, butter lamps flickering in the shadows, incense coiling up towards the ceiling and initiate monks chanting or carving intricate floral butter sculptures in the courtyard. Look for the elusive *takin*, the lovechild between a goat and an antelope, and take in the views of tier upon tier of flooded rice paddies reflecting the sun like shards of a shattered mirror.

This is a place without fences, full of fresh air and fluttering prayer flags, that will reinvigorate your spiritual side and prove you don't need mod cons to feel rich in life.

ABOVE *Make a wish – an old man spinning his prayer wheel.*

RIGHT *Novice monk strolling the grounds of Tashichho Dzong on the northern edge of Thimphu.*

Live like a castaway on a Chilean island

ROBINSON CRUSOE ISLAND, CHILE

Maroon yourself on this historic island that arches like a dolphin through the broad blue of the South Pacific

Stranded 676km (420 miles) off the coast of Chile, Robinson Crusoe Island is built from layers of lava-flow that rise up to form a jagged backbone of mist-shrouded mountains; from these sheer walls cascade silver skeins of waterfalls. It is a seemingly mythical landscape straight from the pages of a fantasy novel.

Formerly (and ironically) known as *Más a Tierra* (Close to Land), the island was renamed Robinson Crusoe Island by the Chilean president, Eduardo Frei, in 1966 in honour of the protagonist in Daniel Defoe's namesake classic, loosely based on the chronicles of Scottish sailor Alexander Selkirk (see page 54).

Home to around 700 people, who mostly eke out a living fishing for lobster, tuna and salmon, life centres around the one and only settlement, San Juan Bautista. Known simply as *el pueblo* (town), it nestles within the curve of Cumberland Bay on the island's sheltered northeastern side. There are no newspapers here, patchy broadband and no ATMs – just a clutch of restaurants and two breweries, one of which produces a dark stout named after Alexander Selkirk.

The island receives just a thousand visitors a year, so, rather uniquely, you are made to feel like a temporary member of the community rather than a tourist. And a visit here will be helping the local economy. In 2010 the island was hit by a 3-m (10-ft) high tsunami which killed four people and caused widespread destruction (rather hauntingly, a tsunami also occurs in Defoe's book). The island community have mostly rebuilt now, but depend on tourism for their economy.

How to do it: Arturo Merino Benítez International Airport, on the outskirts of Santiago, is the gateway to Chile. From there, regularly scheduled 2.5-hour flights depart for Robinson Crusoe Island. Bear in mind that flights are often cancelled due to inclement weather, so allow for some flexibility in your schedule. After that it is a 1-hour ferry journey to San Juan Bautista, the island's main town, where accommodation is found. UK and US citizens do not require a visa to enter Chile for visits of less than 90 days. Instead, travellers are issued a *Tarjeta de Turismo* (Tourist Card) – keep it safe for your departure.

Best time of year: It is best to visit in January, the driest month.

Statue of Robinson Crusoe on Robinson Crusoe Island, one of the three Juan Fernández Islands.

WHO WAS ROBINSON CRUSOE?

Robinson Crusoe – the adventures of a castaway who spends a third of his lifetime stranded on a remote tropical island – was published in 1719 to great acclaim. At first, readers were led to believe that Robinson Crusoe was a real person, but in truth the author, Daniel Defoe, based the character on a mixture of real-life events – most notably the life of Scottish sailor Alexander Selkirk – and fiction.

The story goes that when Selkirk docked at the uninhabited *Más a Tierra* (as Robinson Crusoe Island was once known), he quarrelled with his captain regarding the seaworthiness of their leaky ship *Cinque Ports* and requested to be left ashore. The captain happily agreed and sailed away, leaving Selkirk with just a machete, a musket, a cooking vessel, a knife and a Bible. Incredibly, Selkirk survived for four years and four months – living off lobster, feral goats and fruits – before being rescued in 1709 by William Dampier – part-time pirate and the first British naturalist to explore Australia.

You can hike up to Selkirk's look-out, where he allegedly spent hours scanning the horizon for ships that might rescue him, as well as to his cave-home on Puerto Ingles beach. You can duck into the grottoes where British and Dutch pirates once hid from Spanish ships that were hot on their heels after the theft of treasure, or visit the crumbling remains of 18th-century forts strewn with old artillery. However, the real draw is the unfettered nature.

The island's steep sides give rise to a tight mix of habitats – from coastal and grassland to forest and montane – in an area equivalent to 9,196 football pitches. As a result the range of native plant species rivals that of the Galápagos – 149 in total, of which 91 are endemic – and it is designated a UNESCO World Biosphere Reserve. Look out for the ginger flash of one of the world's rarest birds, the Juan Fernandez Firecrown hummingbird.

Pass your days meandering on horseback, your steed's mane flowing in the wind; dive around the German shipwreck *Dresden* guarded by moray eels and spend time in the quiet company of fish-leather artisans.

Robinson Crusoe Island offers a chance to get away from the hustle and bustle of the real world. At times, it has been described as a lonely place, but in the words of Jean-Paul Sartre: 'If you're lonely when you're alone, you're in bad company.'

A bird's eye view of Robinson Crusoe Island.

TOP TIP

To reach Antarctica, boats must run the gauntlet of the Drake Passage – one of the most treacherous stretches of water in the world because it marks the convergence of the Pacific and Atlantic Oceans. Waves here can tower 12-m (40-ft) high and give rise to the famous 'Drake Shake' that can claim even the sturdiest of stomachs. Happily, the new *Roald Amundsen* is fitted with a narrower hull (compared to standard ships), so can cut through waves more smoothly and reduce the chance of seasickness. Nonetheless, come prepared. The ship's doctor will be on hand to dole out standard seasickness tablets, but other methods worth trying include sucking on ginger sweets, using pressure-point wristbands or – for those that are particularly prone to motion sickness – Scopoderm patches (available on prescription).

Watch icebergs waltz amid the frigid southern seas.

But now, Amundsen's dream has come true (almost). In 2020, the world's first hybrid cruise ship set sail, and it's called the *MS Roald Amundsen*. It uses a combination of low-sulphur diesel and battery power that reduces fuel consumption by 20 per cent. It's not perfect, but it is a step in the sustainable direction. It also allows for closer wildlife encounters: a leopard seal resting on an ice floe is usually scared away by the juddering echoes of a ship's engine long before you can catch a glimpse, but a silent approach buys trust and a better view of the creatures from the ship's deck.

Sailing soundlessly through the fjords and bays reveals Antarctica's serenity. Passing 15,000-year-old icebergs you can't help but feel small, humbled and gifted with a renewed sense of perspective. Don't be alarmed if you struggle to sum up the experience to family and friends on your return. According to guides who lead travellers to the ice-capped continent: 'If you are able to describe Antarctica using words, you probably haven't been there,' – so otherworldly is its charm.

Like so many beautiful things, the continent is deceptively fragile. The threats of over-tourism, fishing, mining and bioprospecting are ever present and responsible travel to this unique place on Earth is crucial to helping it survive; choosing sustainable options where possible, treading lightly while on land, and practising eco-friendly lifestyles back home to slow the global warming that threatens to melt the 5-km (3-mile) deep ice sheet.

Sometimes fighting for silence requires speaking up.

ISLAND IDYLLS

'The starry sky is the truest friend in life, when you've first become acquainted; it is ever there, it gives ever peace, ever reminds you that your restlessness, your doubt, your pains are passing trivialities. The universe is and will remain unshaken. Our opinions, our struggles, our sufferings are not so important and unique, when all is said and done.'

FRIDTJOF NANSEN

Stargaze in one of the darkest places on Earth

AOTEA, GREAT BARRIER ISLAND, NEW ZEALAND

THE LOWDOWN

How to do it: Auckland International Airport is the gateway to New Zealand. From there, Barrier Air operates daily 30-minute flights to Aotea. Discover the World offers tailor-made visits. It's best to book accommodation and car hire in advance. Most travellers don't require a visa but should apply for a New Zealand Electronic Travel Authority pass (NZeTA) online prior to travel.

Best time of year: It's best to visit in winter (June–September) when the angles of the Earth allow you to see the full spread of the Milky Way and you don't have to stay up too late for it to get dark. Otherwise, the new moon offers the darkest skies.

Let the stars unlock a new side of New Zealand

Described by locals as, 'a part of New Zealand that happily forgot to get on the train to the future', Aotea, also known as Great Barrier Island, remains completely off-grid. Located a 30-minute flight northeast of Auckland, the 950 permanent residents who live on this idyll of steep forested hills, farmlands and sweeping white-sand bays power their lives by sun, wind or generator. Seventy per cent of the island is a protected nature reserve. There are no streetlights or billboards, broadband is very limited and phone signal is patchy – welcome to a land without crime, queues, hurry or worries.

All this lack of light pollution makes for a very sparkly stratosphere. 'Here, the stars are so bright you can read the newspaper at night,' laughs local Hilde Hoven. In 2017, the island was designated a Dark Sky Sanctuary because its black night skies offer exceptional views of space. In fact, when the readings were sent off to apply for Dark Sky status, the International Dark-Sky Association (IDA) 'replied to tell us that our skies are dark beyond measurement,' Hoven says.

To give you a sense of what that means: 'It's estimated that in Europe you can only see an average of 500 stars with the naked eye, out here you can see 5,000,' boasts Hoven. This includes constellations unique to the southern hemisphere, such as the Southern Cross and the Magellanic Clouds (dwarf galaxies orbiting the Milky Way) and new ways of seeing the familiar, such as the Pleiades star cluster, or, Seven Sisters on Orion's shoulder, known by its Maori name of Matariki. Look out too for Scorpio's tail, known as Maui's fishhook.

It has been reported that 99 per cent of Americans and Europeans can no longer see the Milky Way due to light pollution. Fabio Falchi, a researcher at the Light Pollution Science and Technology Institute (ISTIL) in Thiene, Italy, believes that as a result, 'we have lost the connection with our roots, of literature, of philosophy, of science, of religion – [because] all are connected with the contemplation of the night sky.'

Marvel at the Milky Way's majesty on Great Barrier Island, New Zealand.

ALSO TRY

Sark, Channel Islands, UK: Suspended between Guernsey and Jersey off the French coast of Normandy, this wildflower-strewn car-free isle was declared the world's first IDA Dark Sky Island. Its twinkly skies are best seen between September and April two hours after sunset.

Møn and Nyord, Denmark: Joined by a bridge, these two rural sister islands in southern Denmark were the first destination in Scandinavia to win IDA Dark Sky status. Stand on the famed white cliffs of Møn and see the stars reflected in the sea, while searching for the Andromeda galaxy.

Isle of Coll, Scotland: One of two IDA Dark Sky sites in Scotland – the other is Galloway Forest Park, a 1.5-hour drive south of Glasgow – this community in the Inner Hebrides is best visited in deep winter because its northern location means summer skies don't get very dark for long.

Soak up the wild panorama of Mount Heale, taken from Mount Hobson, on Great Barrier Island, New Zealand.

So soak up stories about Maori heroes forever immortalized in star formations, or just sit back and survey twinklers the colour of rubies and sapphires as they dance in the deep darkness.

Local certified guides run a variety of experiences ranging from one-and-a-half hours to three hours, with options such as a rustic gourmet dinner, or astro-photography lessons in the wee hours of the morning. Most advise star-gazers not to look at their phones for a good hour beforehand; the white light destroys our night vision.

During the day, you can put boot to soil and attempt one of the 20 trails that criss-cross the quiet island passing natural hot springs, waterfalls and swimming holes, as well as former whaling station sites and Hirakimatā (the island's highest point, also known as Mount Hobson). Other options include nature-focused bush walks, paddleboarding, surfing and horseback hacks past the delicate tendrils of ferns unfurling or the orange-and-purple spray of bird-of-paradise flowers.

In the past, Aotea has traditionally been a summer escape for visitors and the colder winter months were financially lean for locals. However, the IDA Dark Sky status is slowly changing that. It encourages the island's continued reduction in light pollution, conservation and provides employment for the younger generation instead of losing them to the mainland in search of work. It goes against the grain, but for Aotea, the future is dark.

Stroll the soft curve of Medlands Beach, Great Barrier Island.

Unplug in Norway's best-kept secret

SENJA ISLAND, NORWAY

Explore a little-visited corner of the Land of the Midnight Sun

How to do it: Senja is a long way north of Oslo (driving it would take 24 hours), so the quickest way to reach it is a 1.5-hour internal flight from the capital into Bardufoss which is a 1-hour drive from Senja crossing the Gisund Bridge. Alternatively, you can fly into Tromsø and take the 50-minute boat trip to the towns of Finnsnes or Lysnes on Senja. Tour operator Hurtigruten offers round trips of Senja, Andøya and Lofoten.

Best time of year: It may have beaches, but Senja is not a sunny destination. Temperatures hover around -4°C (25°F) in the winter (though it can feel colder due to the wind) and rise to a not-so-balmy 14°C (57°F) at the height of summer. From mid-May to the end of July, the island is ruled by the midnight sun, while the winter months of October, February and March offer increased chances of seeing the northern lights.

Norway is already synonymous with fresh air and rugged vistas but travel to Senja, in the country's far northern fjords, and you enter an even more epic *Lord of the Rings*-esque landscape of jaw-dropping beauty. Nestled between Tromsø to the east and the Lofoten archipelagos to the west, this little-visited island is perhaps Norway's best-kept secret.

With a population hovering around 8,000, Norway's second-largest island has very few shops, and tales of trolls spill liberally from the lips of locals, which all provides plenty of opportunity to disconnect from your harried life and unleash your inner Viking.

Senja's wild western side is a jostle of steep mountains that tower above fishing hamlets of red-clad houses huddled along flat-bottomed valleys; its sheltered east is home to farming and 600-year-old forests. Currently in the process of being certified as a sustainable destination that preserves nature and the environment, Senja is a wrinkled map waiting to be explored.

For a week or more you can sever yourself from your social-media-dominated life and set off on a summer hike through Ånderdalen National Park, home of the iconic Segla peak – a soaring 640-m (2,100-ft) tall column of rock overlooking the freezing sapphire-blue waters of Mefjorden and Ørnfjorden fjords. Look out for moose and semi-wild reindeer amid the pine-clad foothills of the park.

Stroll along Ersfjordstranda's deserted white sandy beach and kayak beneath the midnight sun watching for the ripple of otters and seals. Meet a host of local characters who can teach you about coastal foraging, deep-sea fishing, ocean bathing and felt workshops. Take the time to sample regional delicacies, such as cod from Senja, goat's cheese from Balsfjorden and char from Altevatn Lake. Come winter, you

Camp in the shadow of Segla,
Senja's most iconic peak, Norway.

ALSO TRY

South Koster Island, Sweden: Three hours from the Norwegian capital Oslo, Sweden's sunniest spot sits within a nature reserve and offers local seafood, seals, and wild swimming. The Swedes call it *smultronställe* (a wild strawberry spot), as a way of describing this sweet quiet haven.

Marathi, Greece: This often-unheard-of island has no roads or shops and is Greece's least populated public island with a community of three – the Emilianos family – who accept nine guests at their simple hotel, Pantelis, during the summer.

Juist, Germany: Nicknamed Töwerland (Wonder Land) by locals, this car-free slip of an isle off the coast of northwest Germany has long sandy beaches, honking hordes of seals and is a popular stopping-off point for migratory birds.

The 'Devil's Jaw' or Tungeneset mountain peaks of Senja, Norway.

can try husky sledding, or cross-country skiing and snowshoeing through serene scenes of white and, best of all, you have a really good chance of seeing the *aurora borealis* (northern lights) – far more so here than around Oslo. Try the viewpoints at Bergsbotn or Tungeneset, where the 'Devil's Jaw' Oksen mountain range makes for a dramatic backdrop. Or better yet, try viewing them while bubbling away in an open-air hot tub in the main town of Hamn.

Be sure to visit Husøy, where every afternoon locals have a siesta – a tradition brought to Senja by Spanish sailors centuries ago – and Kaperdalen, one of the best-preserved Sami settlements in Norway. The peat dens, dating from 1900, belonged to the descendants of the Sami, an indigenous group of fast-dwindling semi-nomadic reindeer-herders who once roamed across Norway, Sweden, Finland and Russia.

Do not miss a stay on Tranøya, a secluded private island off Senja's southern coast known for its ancient Viking graves and enveloped in quiet because there are no motorized vehicles except the local farm's tractor. That farm and the old vicarage are run by two sisters who grew up here and returned after careers in teaching and nursing. They run a simple guesthouse and, in addition to serving up scrumptious local food, their aim is to 'create an environment that inspires us to reflect on all the things we are in danger of losing when we allow pace to take control of our life', and allow guests to 'hit the pause button'.

Peaceful places to lay your head include Kråkeslottet (the Crow's Castle) – a wooden fishing plant from 1899 that hovers on stilts above the fjord and is brimming with original features, plus a sauna and grand piano.

Senja is a place to enjoy small, simple pleasures such as spotting an elk or eagle, gliding along the mirror-calm surface of the fjord on a paddleboard, relaxing in a hammock with a good book, or just listening to the eternal wind and waves. It is a real El Dorado.

Go bathing off Crow's Castle, Kråkeslottet, Senja, Norway.

Time travel on this little British outpost

ST HELENA, SOUTH ATLANTIC

How to do it: Titan Airways currently operates a limited chartered flight from London Stansted via Accra in Ghana to St Helena. SA Airlink may resume its weekly 6-hour flight from Johannesburg and its mid-week flight from Cape Town during peak season. Check its website for updates. Accommodation and car hire availability on the island is limited and should be booked well in advance via St Helena Tourism, or a tour operator.

Best time of year: St Helena is best visited between November and March, when days are warm and sunny. There are fewer visitors between April and October, but it is noticeably cooler and wetter. There is also quite a variation on the island itself between the warmer lowlands around Jamestown and the humid wet highlands.

There's a lot to set this island 'Bona-aparte' from others

A volcanic pebble dropped in the vast blue swathe of the frisky South Atlantic Ocean, St Helena is an emerald isle – one of the most isolated on Earth – that combines raw nature with a slow-as-honey lifestyle reminiscent of old-style Britannia. Mist-laced razor-tooth peaks and seas of swaying flax are juxtaposed with one-street villages, and cake and tea. Keys are left in car ignitions, front doors are not locked, and people send each other messages via the local radio station, Saint FM.

A British Overseas Territory, St Helena is a small 16-km (10-mile) wide island with a lot of history. Naturalist Charles Darwin, explorer Captain James Cook, novelist William Thackeray and astronomer Edmond Halley have all stayed here. But its most famous resident was Napoleon Bonaparte, exiled here until his last breath inside elegant Longwood House – you can visit his tomb.

First discovered by the Portuguese in 1502, arrivals had to traverse thousands of miles of restless waves to reach St Helena, creating a seafaring tradition that remained unchanged for hundreds of years. Locals – known as Saints – are the descendants of a mish-mash mix of bloodlines (and accents) of the settlers, soldiers and slaves that farmed, were posted or brought here on those boats.

This tradition ended three years ago when a new airport arrived. It may have shrunk the journey time from five days to six hours, but happily the pace of life has not hurried up. The hurricane of news that the rest of us are exposed to daily does not swirl here. Nothing is rushed. Clothes ordered online can take months to arrive, mobile phone coverage is only five years old and patchy, and Wi-Fi is only found in a handful of houses in the capital, Jamestown.

Longwood House, where Napoleon Bonaparte lived out his exile until his death in 1821, St Helena.

A stay here offers the chance to unplug and unwind not just with massages in the spa, but a deeper reconnection with rewilded nature. Immerse yourself in glass-clear water by diving in reefs full of fish, or gliding along its surface astride a surfboard, paddleboard or a kayak. Take self-guided walks through forests filled with birds or soak up velvet night skies salted with stars. A tranquil emerald Eden to soothe the soul.

ALSO TRY

Silhouette Island, Seychelles: North Island's nearest neighbour is a hub of biodiversity both on- and offshore: with vibrant reefs, healthy populations of giant tortoises and caves cackling with the endangered Seychelles sheath-tailed bat.

Praslin Island, Seychelles: The Seychelles' second-largest island is home to the UNESCO-listed Vallée de Mai, a prehistoric forest that hides the shy endemic black parrot as well as Anse Georgette (*anse* means cove), a pristine smile of sand inside the five-star grounds of the Constance Lemuria hotel, and the family-friendly beach Anse Lazio famed as the best sunset spot on the island.

La Digue, Seychelles: Characterized by laidback family-run guesthouses and offering a slice of real island life, sleepy La Digue is famous for the Instagrammed-to-death Anse Source d'Argent beach. For a more tranquil beach experience, intrepid travellers willing to undertake a steep sweaty forest hike will find the little-visited crystal-clear waters of Anse Marron.

Stay on England's 'Puffin Island'

LUNDY, ENGLAND, UK

Visit this grass-carpeted speck of rock lying ten miles off the Devonshire coast in the Bristol Channel

Lundy is an island fond of single digits, with one pub, one shop, one church, one farmer, one road and one thousand acres of unspoilt nature. There are no cars, no internet, phone reception is patchy, and the only village has no name, well, because it's the only place to go. Fog is such a frequent visitor though that Lundy needed three lighthouses on a stretch of land barely three-miles long and half-a-mile wide.

But don't let size fool you. Men have tussled over this emerald maiden for centuries. Used by the Knights Templar, barbary pirates and smugglers, Lundy was eventually won by two gentlemen in a card game and passed through a succession of private owners until a millionaire bought it and gifted it to the National Trust in 1969.

At least two of those owners took the 'king of my own kingdom' idiom a step too far. In 1235, William de Marisco murdered a messenger of Henry III, fled here and built a castle with three-metre thick walls, but still lost his head; and in the 1920s English businessman, Martin Harman, bought the island and tried to issue his own coinage, which the House of Lords quickly put an end to.

Today, the 27 staff of the Landmark Trust who live on and manage the island aren't quite so territorial. There's even a selection of quirky places to stay, including Marisco's 13th-century castle, a Georgian gentleman's villa and a fisherman's chalet. None of them has a TV, radio or telephone and the electricity is turned off between midnight and 6am, leaving hours of device-free bliss to let yourself also switch off.

Billed as Britain's own Galápagos, Lundy is teeming with creatures great and small. It was named 'Lund-ey', meaning 'Puffin Island' by marauding Vikings, which is a bit of

The dramatic Hartland Peninsula on Lundy, UK.

How to do it: From the end of March until the end of October, the MS *Oldenburg* – a union-jack-flying wood-panelled 1950s vessel that brings supplies to the island – sails up to four times a week from either Ilfracombe or Bideford on the UK mainland. Sailing time is under 2 hours and tickets should be pre-booked. During winter (November–March), you'll need to book a 7 minute flight via helicopter that runs from Monday to Friday from Hartland Point. Alternatively, if you have your own sails or wings, you can land on Lundy for a small fee.

Best time of year: The long, calm, warm-weather days of summer are best for two reasons: one, puffin season runs from the end of March until the end of August and two, ferry tickets are half the price of helicopter flights, which are the only option of getting here in winter.

ALSO TRY

Farne Islands, England, UK: Archipelago off the coast of Northumberland with guaranteed sightings of puffins – the colony is 43,000 strong – and grey seals, which travel here every autumn to pup. Twitchers will be in a tizz thanks to the 22 other species of seabird that whirl around the shorelines.

Jura, Inner Hebrides, Scotland, UK: George Orwell sequestered himself on this remote mountainous isle in the 1940s to write *Nineteen Eighty-Four*. Locals number around 200 and are hugely outnumbered by the thousands of deer that roam its bogs. After a wind-whipped walk you can ward off the chill with a dram of the island's local whisky.

Bardsey Island, Wales: Billed by medieval bards as 'the land of indulgences, absolution and pardon, the road to Heaven, and the gate to Paradise', the island of Ynys Enlli is purportedly the resting place of 20,000 saints – not forgetting Merlin, King Arthur's wizard – but today it has only four permanent (living) residents. Meaning you have plenty of solitude to stare up at the sea-bird-filled sky or spot dolphins, porpoises and grey seals.

a spoiler for those that didn't know around 400 of these clown-eyed fishers of sand eels turn up every summer to nest. Other highlights include the trunk-nosed pygmy shrew – the UK's smallest land mammal – as well as pipistrelle bats and introduced sika deer and highland cattle. Each season brings new small things to notice, if you take the time.

You'll need to look to the sea and undertake a snorkel safari to discover all of the magic. The area was designated in 2010 as England's first Marine Conservation Zone, rich in cold water corals. The converging currents of the Atlantic Ocean and the Bristol Channel stir up a soup of nutrient-rich waters that attract species such as basking sharks, leatherback turtles and sunfish, which can grow to be 4-m (13-ft) long. You can also spot minke and long-finned pilot whales, porpoises, several species of dolphin and sunbathing Atlantic grey seals.

Finally, you can't leave Lundy without trying letterboxing. This activity (also possible on St Helena, see page 84) is a treasure trail of 27 hidden letterboxes scattered around the island in off-the-beaten-track locations that need to be found using clues and a compass. Each letterbox contains a rubber stamp which participants use to mark their 'letterboxing' book purchased from the local shop – most challenging of all is the 'Lundy Bunny', the movable stamp. It's a peaceful pursuit that entices all family members away from their screens and opens their eyes instead to the many wild charms of Lundy.

FAR LEFT *The old lighthouse and keeper's cottage on Lundy, UK.*

LEFT) *Puffin on Lundy's cliffs.*

Savour a good vintage and watch for whales in the Azores

PICO ISLAND, AZORES

A trip that combines nature watching with wine tasting engages all your senses

Pico looks like an island a child would draw: a jostle of green surrounded by cyan seas and crowned by a towering conical volcano. It's impossible not to have your breath just a little bit arrested by the sight of the sometimes-snow-capped Ponta do Pico – Portugal's highest mountain at 2,351m (7,713ft) – that rises like a rugged guardian above the island's whitewashed villages and high cliffs that plunge into foamy blue seas.

At just 300,000 years old, Pico is the baby of the Azores – an exposed archipelago 1,400km (870 miles) off the coast of Portugal – and was the last to be inhabited by a mixture of Portuguese settlers, African slaves and exiled Jews and, thanks to its continued low population, it retains its wildness.

Portuguese poet, Raul Brandão, called it *Ilha Preta* (Black Island) in reference to its basalt-block houses and jostle of ebony lava fields. From this seemingly desolate landscape settlers devised an ingenious growing technique: they hand-crafted *currais*, basalt-walled allotments that sheltered grape vines from the frisky Atlantic winds and trapped heat that kept the fruits warm overnight. The result was a unique form of viniculture that produced much lauded *verdelho* wines that graced the dining tables of Russian czars. Volcanic eruptions and disease almost wiped them out, but the tradition has slowly been revived and in 2004 won the island UNESCO status. The best examples of the unusual allotments can be seen around Criação Velha, Santa Luzia and São Mateus and you can learn more at the Paisagem da Cultura da Vinha da Ilha do Pico. Join a full-day wine tour and remind yourself how the simple act of sipping and savouring a good vintage causes you to slip into a slower gear and reconnect you with the Earth.

THE LOWDOWN

How to do it: TAP and Azore Airlines offer direct flights from Lisbon on the Portuguese mainland. Alternatively, Atlânticoline ferries runs multiple daily sailings from the neighbouring islands of Faial and São Jorge to the port of Madalena on Pico. Despite its diminutive size there are a handful of hotels and AirBnB rentals.

Best time of year: The weather in the Azores is fickle and famed for its four seasons in one day. As a rough guide, May to September are the driest months and best for calmer waters for boat tours; they also coincide with the whale migrations.

A sperm whale starts a deep dive off the coast of Pico in the Azores.

Comino, Malta: Pirates once stashed their treasure amid the many caves of this tiny island. Today, it's a nature reserve and bird sanctuary, with ancient towers and chapels, one hotel and a permanent population of just two – leaving plenty of space for you and nature.

Hiddensee, Germany: Nicknamed *Söte Länneken* (Sweet Little Isle) by locals, this wood-and-dunes whisker of land in the Baltic Sea is completely car-free. Horse-drawn carriage is still the main mode of transport for the island's 1,000 inhabitants, who will infuse you with their calm carefree attitude to life.

Procida, Italy: Reachable only by ferry, this bijou isle was named Italian Capital of Culture in 2022 and lies off the coast around Naples. Procida was the star of *The Talented Mr Ripley* movie thanks to its medieval walled village filled with sorbet-coloured homes. It's a place for creatives to read and write, inspired by the sea view and sipping *aperitivos*.

Pico is not a white-sand beach escape – in fact, there are no beaches. Instead, there are lakes feathered by migratory birds; Gruta das Torres, one of the longest lava tubes in the world; volcanic arches and caves; and a spirited sea that can calm even the most restless of hearts.

Here, the old ways live on. Especially in places such as Santo Amaro parish, where boats are still built by hand, locals handcraft flowers out of fish scales and octopus is stewed in wine with taro root.

Pico Island's baleen-like shape hints at its other attraction – whales. More than 20 species – from the humpback whale to the migratory blue whale (the world's biggest animal) – arc through the Azores' blue waters, making it one of the very best places in the world for whale watching. In the past, this abundance attracted many hunters who patrolled the seas, particularly for sperm whales, until 1987. The ports of São Roque and Lajes are still lined with old whaler homes and both have museums detailing that darker past.

Today, the only shooting that takes place is with a camera. By protecting the whales, the island has reinvented itself as a model for sustainable tourism and one of the best ecotourism destinations in Europe. From mid-March to the end of October, sail out and revel in the silence that descends as a boat of people collectively hold their breath listening on the wind for the puff of air from a whale's blowhole.

LEFT *Hand-crafted* currais *walls made of lava rock built to shelter the vines, Pico, Azores.*

BELOW *Trekking on Pico.*

Enjoy hospitality and horizons on Fogo

FOGO, NEWFOUNDLAND AND LABRADOR, CANADA

Discover the island of bracing winds and warm, warm hearts

'Fogo is not so much a place, as a state of mind,' says *National Geographic* journalist Robin Esrock. An island within an island, this hard-to-reach outpost on the far eastern fringes of Canada seems to exist outside of time. It boasts seven seasons (rather than the usual four) and a rock that members of the Flat Earth Society have claimed is one of the four corners of the Earth. Exposed to the unforgiving Atlantic on three sides, it feels as if on Fogo the air is fresher, the wind sharper, the horizon broader and your sense of being keener.

But don't let this rugged exterior fool you; the heart of a tight-knit coastal community beats warmly here. Made up of just over 2,200 people spread across 11 villages, these 'Newfies' (the nickname given to Newfoundland residents) are the descendants of English Protestants from Devon and Dorset and Catholics from southeast Ireland – and they have a fruit salad of an accent and dialect to prove it.

Much like the indigenous Beothuk people, their fiercely independent forebears survived by hunting, foraging and fishing the cod-rich seas and rarely mixed with 'come from aways' (outsiders). Not much has changed. Locals are a profoundly self-sufficient bunch of 'punt, skiff and bullyboat' builders, master recyclers and artisans whose lives are deeply entangled with nature. And they exude hospitality on a scale many of us have long since lost; quickly striking up a conversation or inviting you into their home – painted bright as Lego bricks – for a plate of salted cod and potatoes.

To hang on to their roots they've had to diversify a little and have established the Fogo Island Inn, a social enterprise that reinvests 100 per cent of its profits back into the community. The island's boat builders applied their skills to make the inn's furniture, and hookers (quilters!) made the bedspreads. Be sure to spend languorous hours bubbling away in the inn's rooftop hot tub and sauna.

THE LOWDOWN

How to do it: Fly into St John's International Airport; some routes arrange a direct connection to Gander Airport, but otherwise you'll need to arrange a separate charter flight or helicopter. From Gander, you need to catch a taxi or hire a car to drive the 1.5 hours to Farewell, where the 45-minute M/V Windsor Ferry departs for Fogo multiple times a day.

Best time of year: Due to its exposed location on the Atlantic coastline, Fogo is best visited in its summer months (July–August) when art exhibitions and other events take place. However, accommodation is open year-round and if you're happy to brave the freezing temperatures and odd blizzard you can see icebergs and explore the snow-covered landscape by snowshoe, snowmobile or toboggan.

Fogo, the largest of the islands off the coast of Newfoundland and Labrador in Canada, is not so much a place as a state of mind.

The ultra-modern Fogo Island Inn has views to savour.

A scheme pairs visitors with a Community Host: passionate islanders that can really help you get to know the secret spots, teach you how to make berry ice cream, or introduce you to customs such as a 'boil up' – an outdoor winter picnic with snacks and tea cooked in a cast-iron kettle over a roaring fire.

Locals have also developed a thriving arts and crafts scene and now offer pottery, painting, drawing, quilting and wood workshops, as well as letting you spend quiet afternoons touring their studios.

But it's hard to ignore the nature that rustles, cracks and calls outside the window. Fogo is located within 'Iceberg Alley', the stretch of Atlantic between Greenland and Newfoundland that's bobbing with icebergs like a crowded drink. And these rich waters bring humpback whales, seals, and flocks of puffins, gannets, eiders and scoters that wheel or bob on the choppy waves.

A wondrous geographical quirk! This island may be located near Newfoundland, but it's actually part of France. They use the euro, munch *tarte au citron* and even the street signs are seemingly pilfered from Paris. It also has its own time zone 30 minutes ahead of Newfoundland. A laidback slice of *la vie plus belle*.

Wrangel Island, Russia: Described by a 19th-century traveller as 'the end of creation' this remote reserve certainly feels like the edge of the world. Special government permission is required to visit, but the wildness and wildlife are worth the effort; polar bear, musk ox, walrus, whales – and even the spiralled tusks of woolly mammoths that survived here 6,000 years longer than everywhere else.

Battle Harbour, Newfoundland and Labrador: Billed as 'Nine miles from Normal' this remote island was the capital of Labrador's saltfish industry for 200 years. It's now a living museum, but travellers can still stay in refurbished homes or a quaint inn and spend peaceful days berry-picking and enjoying bracing windy walks.

There are around 14 hiking trails on the island, stretching for 200km (124 miles) through the untouched forest and heathlands. Look out for endangered caribou, fox, coyote and beavers as you pass geological contortions of rock forged by ice, fire and sea, and melancholy abandoned communities such as Eastern Tickle and Lion's Den. Even the more high-octane activities can be enjoyed in silence, including snowmobiling under the stars and seal watching. Then end your day seated around a crackling campfire swapping stories and songs. As you'd say in Fogo lingo: it really 'dies at ya', (you'll really, really like it).

Immerse yourself in myths and mystical landscapes

HAIDA GWAII, CANADA

Soak-up this remote, time-forgotten, rain-cloaked land

How to do it: Air Canada and Pacific Coastal Airlines operate flights from Vancouver to Sandpit and Masset on Haida Gwaii. Alternatively, BC Ferries operates a year-round 8-hour car ferry from Prince Rupert, on the mainland, to Skidegate on Haida Gwaii. Accommodation should be pre-booked and it's worth renting a car. Guests can stay in a range of timber-clad guesthouses, or the highly recommended Haida House.

The only slice of Canada to escape the last Ice Age, Haida Gwaii is a place of shape-shifting deities, clans people divided into eagles and ravens, and where there's talk of a spruce tree with golden needles.

A hundred miles off the coast of northern British Columbia, the archipelago is made up of two main islands – Graham and Moresby – and a smattering of 148 other islets. Formerly known as the Queen Charlotte Islands, or Charlottes, it changed its name in 2010 to honour the ancestry of the indigenous Haida people who have lived here for 13,000 years and still represent half of the 5,000-strong population.

Best time of year: Make no mistake, Haida Gwaii is a wet place. It boasts the honour of holding three locations in the Top Ten Rainiest Places in British Columbia – receiving up to 4,000mm (157.5in) of rainfall annually. Temperatures average around 7°C (45°F). Your best chance for fresh, sunny days fall between May to mid-September, but pack your waterproofs regardless.

The Haida are a nation of artists; the great Bill Reid's 'Spirit of Haida Gwaii' carving is featured on the back of the Canadian $20-bill. And while ancient customs and practices – such as plant medicine, stringing seashell-necklaces and speaking Haida, a unique language with no known root to any other, are fading – there are still strong Haida communities on the islands, most notably at HlGaagilda (Skidegate) at the south end of Graham Island and Gaw Tlagee (Old Massett) in the north. There are also around 500 archaeological sites on the islands, most important among them is the UNESCO-listed Sgang Gwaii, a village of wooden longhouses in use until the 1880s and home to the world's oldest original standing totem poles. It sits within the hard-to-reach Gwaii Haanas National Park, which has no signage, roads or structures and is accessible only by kayak, seaplane or boat. These are places to soak up age-old knowledge and deep silence.

However, the islands' charms aren't just cultural. Known as the 'Galápagos of the North' this bio-rich environment of moss-laced spruce and giant red cedars, some over 1,000 years old, is home to pine martens, shrews, beavers and the world's largest black bears. Off the rugged rocky coastline, the warm Alaska current attracts shoals of salmon and herring, which lure bald eagles and up to a million seabirds, as well as

Totem pole depicting clan membership in otherworldly Haida Gwaii, British Columbia, Canada.

sea lions, porpoise, dolphin, otter and seven species of whale, including grey, orca and humpbacks. Set out on a kayak and quite often you'll come within metres of these marine giants; the only sound being the occasional puff and sneeze as they exhale, and the peaceful dribble and plop of your oar cutting through silk-smooth waters of the sheltered inlets.

Life here is intimately connected with the sea, both economically and spiritually, and you'll experience a strange serenity as you stroll along the wild sandy driftwood-strewn beaches of Naikoon Provincial Park, hunting for treasured quartz on Agate Beach, or joining locals for a spot of ocean cleansing (cold water dips).

Inland, spend quiet hours visiting the galleries and studios where Haida artists carve canoes and poles. Join local guides to forage for thimbles, huckleberries, mushrooms, mussels, clams and sea asparagus and dine on Haida meals of kelp, sea urchin and crab, and share in a potlatch (a traditional celebration). And last of all, trace the Golden Spruce Trail, where the famous Kiidk'yaas – a sacred spruce tree with a rare genetic mutation that turned its needles golden – stood until 1997.

BELOW *Orcas are frequent visitors to the waters around Haida Gwaii.*

RIGHT *Haida Gwaii's rugged terrain is rich in indigenous mythology.*

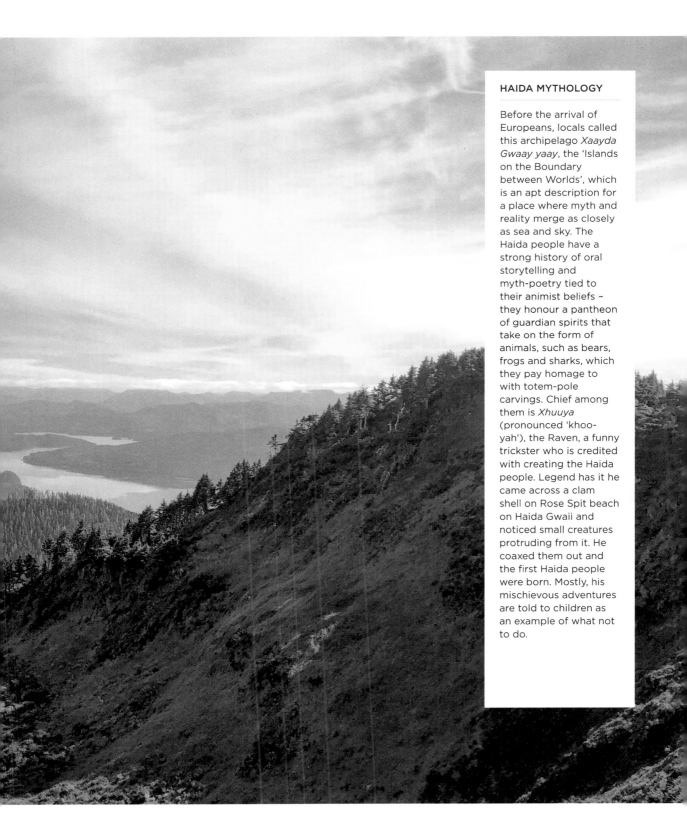

HAIDA MYTHOLOGY

Before the arrival of Europeans, locals called this archipelago *Xaayda Gwaay yaay*, the 'Islands on the Boundary between Worlds', which is an apt description for a place where myth and reality merge as closely as sea and sky. The Haida people have a strong history of oral storytelling and myth-poetry tied to their animist beliefs – they honour a pantheon of guardian spirits that take on the form of animals, such as bears, frogs and sharks, which they pay homage to with totem-pole carvings. Chief among them is *Xhuuya* (pronounced 'khoo-yah'), the Raven, a funny trickster who is credited with creating the Haida people. Legend has it he came across a clam shell on Rose Spit beach on Haida Gwaii and noticed small creatures protruding from it. He coaxed them out and the first Haida people were born. Mostly, his mischievous adventures are told to children as an example of what not to do.

SOULFUL CONTEMPLATION

'In a world that entices us to browse through the lives of others to help us better determine how we feel about ourselves, and to in turn feel the need to be constantly visible — for visibility these days seems to somehow equate to success — don't be afraid to disappear...and see what comes to you in silence.'

MICHAELA COEL

Experience life on the edge of the world

FOULA, SHETLAND ISLANDS, UK

The UK's most remote, permanently inhabited island offers complete liberation from everyday life

How to do it: First, travel to Aberdeen, Glasgow, Edinburgh or Inverness then catch a Loganair flight to Sumburgh Airport. Then travel 40 minutes north to Tingwall Airport to catch a 15-minute Airtask flight. Alternatively, Northlink Ferries offers an overnight departure seven nights a week from Aberdeen to Lerwick. Then it's a 30-minute drive across the island to Walls to catch the twice-weekly BK Marine ferry to Foula. Weather frequently disrupts travel, and there are only two self-catering accommodation options available, Burns and Ristie, so book in advance.

Best time of year: Best visited in summer (June–August) when there's a greater chance of mild weather. However, bracing wind, rain and cloud are common all year round – pack accordingly.

Marooned between Norway and mainland Scotland, and on the same latitude as St Petersburg in Russia and Anchorage in Alaska, Foula is a wild hunk of wind-whipped rock just 4km (2.5 miles) wide and 5.5km (3.5 miles) long and home to 38 people. There is no pub, no shop, no public transport and residents only received running water and electricity in the 1980s.

Dominating the island are five peaks with names that could have been lifted straight from the pages of *Lord of the Rings*: Noup, Hamnafield, Sneug, Kame and Soberlie. They drop off to form some of the highest sheer cliffs in the UK, plunging 360m (1,180 ft) into the frothing, foaming waves below.

At the mercy of the wrathful Atlantic, Foula is shrouded in mist and mystery. A place that once spoke Norn (see page 120) and retains its own shorthand for life and living: where ravens are *corbies*, seals are *selkies* and the lichen, Old Man's Beard, is smoked as tobacco when weather disrupts usual deliveries. A place of Bronze-Age burial mounds, old ship and plane wrecks.

Four detailed self-guided walks can be followed, or you can book one of the local rangers to guide you. Highlights include the Gaada sea stack and the neighbouring, now collapsed, Broch Arch that once had an early Christian monastic cell perched atop it where the monks would retreat for solitude and meditation. Come midsummer, the shoreline, moorland and marshes are a riot of wildflowers; the sky alive with meadow pipits, skylarks and wheatears.

Silence on this island doesn't necessarily mean quiet, instead it is interpreted as a space to roam and breathe clean air deeply. For Foula means 'Bird Island' and the squawks, trills and shrill calls of some half a million birds will be the soundtrack to your stay here. Puffins, Arctic terns, red-throated divers, guillemots, shags and

The wrathful Atlantic waves pounding the coastline of Foula in the Scottish Shetland Islands.

LOST LANGUAGE

Foula was one of the last places to speak Norn – an Old Norse dialect with Danish, Faroese, Frisian and Scots words worked into it. The best-surviving example is a 17th-century ballad called *Hildina* detailing the revenge of the King of Norway against the Earl of Orkney for the kidnap of his daughter Hildina. We know of it thanks to a Scottish clergyman, George Low, who travelled in Foula in 1774 to mark down fragments of the already-fading language. When another philologist visited 120 years later, all memory of Norn had been lost.

gannets – birdwatchers can see them all. Observe Arctic skuas defending their chicks against marauding bonxies (great skuas) – Foula has the biggest colony in the world – and watch out for the fulmars spitting foul-smelling oil at you.

Outnumbered by these seabirds thirteen-thousand to one, locals here are a resilient, fiercely independent people who still celebrate Christmas on 6 January because they refused to abandon the Julian calendar when the rest of the country did so in 1752. Once they eked a living from fishing, living off piltaks and potatoes, but today they're mainly crofters living in the hamlets of Hametun and Ham and sharing the island with hundreds of hardy and genetically unique Foula sheep and one-metre (38-in) tall Shetland ponies. Here, the heart of true community still beats, with everyone holding down three or four jobs to keep the island running.

There are just two stone-built croft houses for visitors to stay in. The no-frills Burns on the east of the island, and Ristie in the north, which sleeps up to eight people and overlooks the Gaada stack. What could be better for the soul than coming back from a windswept walk, pouring a dram of whisky, propping your feet up on the Aga to warm, and toasting a visit to the edge of the world.

LEFT *Foula is home to just 38 people and some half-a-million birds.*

BELOW *Arctic skuas spend most of their lives at sea, but come ashore in summer to breed.*

Connect with your inner hermit on a mountainside pilgrimage

SACRED WALKS, ABRUZZO, ITALY

Explore awe-inspiring paths and rock-hewn hermitages

Think of Italy and the mind conjures impassioned yells from baristas and a barrage of honking Vespa horns, but the region of Abruzzo offers a calmer alternative. Two hours east of Rome, this little-known part of Italy is the country's greenest thanks to three national parks that cover a third of its area.

Snaking through the eastern Majella National Park is the 66-km (41-mile) long *Sentiero dello Spirito* (Spirit Trail) – an ancient pilgrimage route connecting medieval chapels, abbeys and rock-hewn hermitages that cling to mountainsides as tightly as swallows' nests. The national park is home to the most holy places per square kilometre (square mile) in the world, outside Tibet.

This is slow Italy, where the old ways still thrive. Where family-run *trattorias* fill you with hand-cut ravioli stuffed with local pecorino sheep cheese and saffron – grown in Abruzzo's plains – washed down with a cheeky glass (or four) of Montepulciano, the regional red wine. Where *nonnas* (grandmothers), garbed in traditional black dresses, sit beneath line-hung laundry, gossiping; and shepherds still haunt the honey-grass plains, while their white Maremma dogs round up the unruly flocks. And through the forests of russet-coloured ferns and hemlock trees roam Marsican brown bears, wolves and wild boars.

It is a trail best traversed using horses to carry essentials. Local horsemen offer their long-fringed Haflinger ponies, who shoulder camping supplies across flaxen meadows, dimpled with purple cornflowers, thistles and *tholos* – circular stone huts dating from the 1800s that were used to store farm tools. Amid these landscapes, you will sleep under canvas and swathes of stars, passing a pot of polenta and mug of wine back and forth across the flickering campfire.

Walking around 10km (6 miles) a day, the route includes Rifugio della Rocca – Europe's highest medieval castle – and Campo Imperatore, a swathe of undulating grassland

How to do it: Hikers can explore the parks and hermitages independently and arrange their own shorter routes. Purchase a detailed hiking map, such as Cicerone's *Walking in Abruzzo*, to help you. However, the area's history is brought to life by specialists such as Sacred Walks which offers a nine-day guided trip with a pick-up and drop-off from Rome Fiumicino Airport. Many national airlines operate direct daily flights to Rome. Hikers cover roughly 10km (6 miles) per day (around 6 hours), so should be fit.

Best time of year: Late April to mid-May is the very best time to walk among the wildflowers, see newborn lambs and enjoy the warming temperatures.

The Hermitage of Sant'Onofrio dates back to the thirteenth century and clings to the mountainside like a swallow's nest, Abruzzo, Italy.

Who was Sant'Onofrio?

Records are patchy, but he is acknowledged as one of the original Desert Fathers – not a rock band, but rather a handful of early Christians who lived in the desert in Egypt around 300AD and risked bandits, starvation and the wrath of the elements to prove their faith to God. Legend has it that on his 17th day of wandering in the wilderness, Paphnutius – a fellow Egyptian ascetic – came across the wild figure of Onofrio, dressed only in a loincloth of leaves. Onofrio took Paphnutius to his rock-hewn cell but died the next morning. Paphnutius buried him amid the rocks, and as he turned to leave Onofrio's cave crumbled.

RIGHT *Statue of a saint hewn by hand into the cliffs.*

OPPOSITE TOP *One of the best ways to explore the countryside, astride local Haflinger ponies.*

OPPOSITE BOTTOM *Known as 'Little Tibet,' the grasslands of Campo Imperatore were actually used as the backdrop of several spaghetti western films.*

2,000m (6,562ft) above sea level nicknamed 'Little Tibet', whose open plains were the ideal budget backdrop for numerous Spaghetti Westerns and the location for *The American* starring George Clooney.

But the highlights are the hermitages. Chiselled from the fossilized fish-and-coral-studded limestone cliffs, these nook-and-cranny places of worship were the work of Catholic hermits and monks who shunned public work to commune with God. Learn of extraordinary characters such as Sant'Onofrio, purportedly the son of the King of Persia, who renounced court and lived in a cave for 70 years with just a loincloth and his long grey hair to keep him warm; or Pietro da Morrone, a humble hermit who rose, gladiator-style, to become Pope in 1294. Sit in the contemplative silence of these starkly beautiful caves as fat candles flicker in the shadows, illuminating small crosses scratched on the walls by long-dead pilgrims. While, on the rough altar, smoky skeins of frankincense snake upwards towards the rocky roof. A pilgrimage through these green lands will fundamentally change your impressions of Italy.

Embrace the Aboriginal wisdom of stillness

KAKADU NATIONAL PARK, AUSTRALIA

THE LOWDOWN

How to do it: Darwin is the closest airport to Kakadu National Park. International travellers may have to fly into one of the other major Australian cities, such as Sydney, first and catch a connecting flight. From Darwin, it's a 3-hour drive on good tarred roads. Visitors require a car to get around the park, or you can join a tour. A park pass (valid for a week) must be purchased online prior to entry.

Best time of year: Summers (November–April) in northern Australia are tropical, with crackling thunderstorms, and torrential rain. Although there are fewer visitors and park passes are cheaper during this time, flooding is a real risk and since the region receives under 200,000 travellers annually anyway, it's best to visit during the dry season (May–October).

Dreamtime, songlines, walkabout

Aboriginal people have been intimately connected to their land for more than 65,000 years. They can hear the whisper of its ancient wisdom and they listen. The Ngan'gikurunggurr people of the Daly River region in Australia's Northern Territory call this deep listening *dadirri* (pronounced 'da-did-ee'). Aboriginal activist and artist Miriam Rose Ungunmerr, from the Nauiyu community, describes this listening for those not brought up in the community: 'There are deep springs within each of us. Within this deep spring, which is the very Spirit of God, is a sound. The sound of Deep calling to Deep. We call on it and it calls to us. It is something like what you call "contemplation".'

She goes on to say, 'In our Aboriginal way, we learnt to listen from our earliest days. We could not live good and useful lives unless we listened. This was the normal way for us to learn – not by asking questions. We learnt by watching and listening, waiting and then acting. My people are not threatened by silence. They are completely at home in it. They have lived for thousands of years with Nature's quietness. My people today, recognize and experience in this quietness, the great Life-Giving Spirit, the Father of us all. Our Aboriginal culture has taught us to be still and to wait. We do not try to hurry things up. We let them follow their natural course – like the seasons.'

Using meaningful silence, the Nauiyu have begun to muffle the long-lasting effects of the Great Australian Silence – a deliberate and sustained effort to stamp out Aboriginal culture from the late-18th until the mid-20th century. Ungunmerr wishes for *balanda* (non-Aboriginal people) to try it and where better than amid one of Australia's richest hubs for Aboriginal culture: the UNESCO-listed Kakadu National Park, the country's largest.

Listen to the 'songlines' sung by the indigenous Arnhem Land on the trek to Jim Jim Falls, Kakadu National Park, Australia.

ALSO TRY

Marquesas Islands, French Polynesia: One of the most remote group of islands in the world, this archipelago is infused with the spirit of its Polynesian ancestors who are represented with giant stone *tiki* – remarkably similar to the *moai* found on Rapa Nui (Easter Island) 3,662km (2,275 miles) away. Visit and learn new ways of connecting with nature.

Ikara-Flinders Ranges National Park, Australia: A 4.5-hour drive north of Adelaide and co-managed by the region's indigenous Adnyamathanha people, this fiery red mountain range has 14 hiking trails ideal for bush walks that connect you to plants, animals and ancient songlines.

Te Rerenga Wairua, New Zealand: Cape Reinga on the most northwestern tip of North Island – where the Tasman Sea meets the Pacific Ocean – is known to the Maori as 'leaping place of the spirits': a broad sandy beach where souls depart Earth for the afterlife and a lighthouse that overlooks nothing but the boundless blue horizon.

Peering over the edge of Twin falls inside Kakadu National Park. During summer, they run dry but during the tropical summer months heavy rains bring them to life.

Situated 160km (100 miles) southeast of Darwin and half the size of Switzerland, this vast landscape of tropical rainforests and rocky plateaus seems almost mythical. Spread between the Alligator Rivers, it's home to quolls, phascogales and bandicoots, has grass that grows 3-m (10-ft) tall and at night the soupy air vibrates with frog song. Among its rocks are 5,000 art sites, including 20,000-year-old rock paintings at Ubirr, Nourlangie and Nanguluwur depicting stories of hunting and sorcery. Stand and feel these stories instead of trying to make linear sense of them.

Go for a walkabout on one of the 30 trails to connect yourself with the land. Swim close to the sky at the Gunlom billabong, a freshwater swimming hole perched above the Kakadu Escarpment that featured in the 1980s classic film *Crocodile Dundee*. Boat out into the lily-laden crocodile-infested Yellow River, or soak in the rainforest-surrounded Maguk rock pools. Sit quietly amid the Mamukala wetlands – visited by millions of migratory birds and home to a third of Australia's 280 bird species – looking out for comb-crested jacanas, purple swamp hens and iridescent kingfishers. And learn the art of painting and weaving from the guardians of these wild timeless lands that hum with life and even music, if you learn to listen.

OPPOSITE *Soak up the soulful sunsets of Kakadu's wetlands.*

ABOVE *Connect with the past observing Aboriginal rock art at Ubirr, Kakadu National Park.*

Retreat into darkness on a journey of self-discovery

KOH PHANGAN, THAILAND

THE LOWDOWN

How to do it: The closest international airport to Koh Phangan is Nakhon Si Thammarat on the mainland. From there, take a bus to Don Sak Pier to catch a 2.5-hour ferry to Koh Phangan. Once on the island you can take a taxi for the 15-minute drive to Srithanu. You'll need to book the dark retreat before you arrive.

Best time of year: Domes can be booked throughout the year, check online (see page 251) for availability.

Cultures around the globe and throughout history have valued the clarity that sitting in total darkness can bring

'Go inside the cave of your own heart. When you can bear and be your own emptiness, you are free,' says Jamaican spiritual teacher, Mooji.

For centuries wise men have retreated into darkness to immerse themselves in silence and access their inner light. From the ancient Egyptians and 15th-century French mystics, to Tibetan Buddhist monks and the 'jaguar' Kogi people of northern Colombia, darkness has been used as a shamanic tool to uncover the true 'self' as it's believed the lack of light stimulates the pineal gland, also known as the 'third eye'.

With no new information to process and store, your brain slowly starts to relax and rest. This enhances clarity and allows those facing fears and trauma the space to heal and rejuvenate, so they can develop trust in their own inner guidance.

In India, the practice of dark retreats is offered as an Ayurvedic medical treatment to slow the ageing process and regain vitality. It is known as Kaya Kalpa, meaning 'immortal body'.

The science behind long periods in darkness shows that during the first three days, the pineal gland releases more melatonin (the sleep hormone) that quiets the nervous system; over the next three days there's an increase in the neurotransmitter pinoline, which encourages dream states and increased conscious awareness; while after six days in darkness, the brain starts synthesizing 5-methoxy-dimethyltryptamine (5-MeO-DMT) and dimethyltryptamine (DMT) that bring on transcendental feelings of universal love. Aficionados believe that the meditative state you reach through these chemical fluctuations brought on by the dark is far deeper than the levels you can reach in daylight. Described as like returning to the womb, it's a chance to strip life back to the basics and cocoon yourself in a perpetual state of night.

So, where to try it? In the jungled hills above Srithanu, on Thailand's fifth biggest island of Koh Phangan, stand two monolith domes built of earth. Completely off grid,

The island of Koh Phangan in Thailand is famed for its beaches, but dark retreats will reveal inner landscapes far richer.

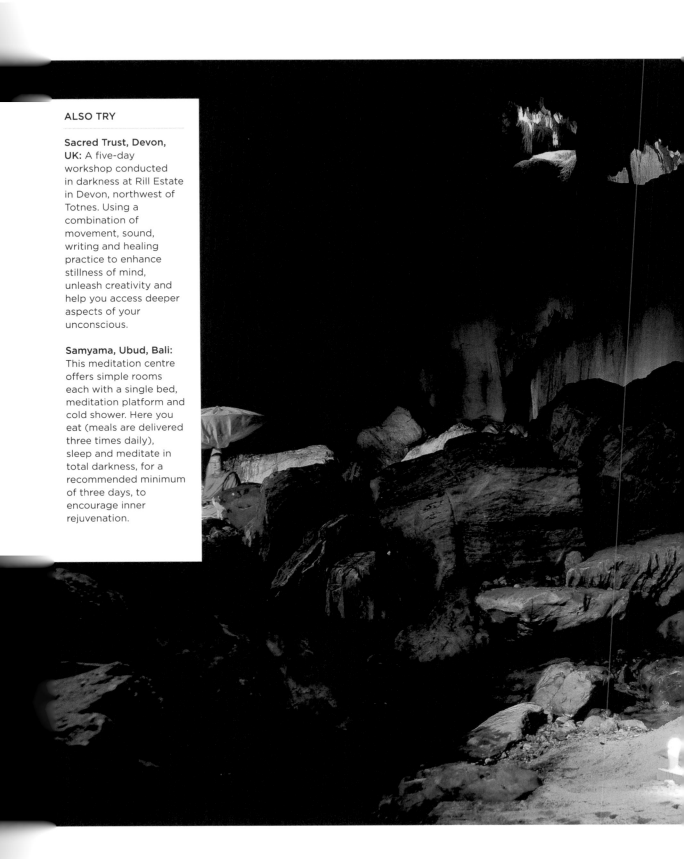

ALSO TRY

Sacred Trust, Devon, UK: A five-day workshop conducted in darkness at Rill Estate in Devon, northwest of Totnes. Using a combination of movement, sound, writing and healing practice to enhance stillness of mind, unleash creativity and help you access deeper aspects of your unconscious.

Samyama, Ubud, Bali: This meditation centre offers simple rooms each with a single bed, meditation platform and cold shower. Here you eat (meals are delivered three times daily), sleep and meditate in total darkness, for a recommended minimum of three days, to encourage inner rejuvenation.

Buddhist monks meditating in the cocooning darkness of a cave.

they are equipped with simple amenities and, while you can still hear the patter of rain, the chirrup of birds and the light strings of crickets, all light is completely sealed out. Owner Santosh, who holds a degree in neuroscience and biochemistry, recommends a minimum of three days.

However, if you have no experience of meditation, or sitting in complete darkness feels too intimidating or claustrophobic, then you can practise the art of staying still as part of a group immersion. These sessions are performed on a raised wooden deck open to the jungle on all sides. You pick a spot, string up your mosquito net, and don't budge. No talking with others, no phones, and ideally you bring enough food with you to avoid trips to local restaurants too. After this introduction into yogic breathing and self-inquiry, you can enter the earth domes if you wish.

Ironically, it seems the first step to 'seeing' who we really are, is to take away our sight for a few days.

Make friends with silence on a Vipassana retreat

VARIOUS LOCATIONS, INDIA

How to do it: Ten-day Vipassana courses are hosted all over India and are usually free of charge to all. All expenses (excluding airfare), including food and accommodation, are met by donations usually offered by attendees who complete the retreat and wish for others to experience the same freedom of mind. Those recommended include: Dhamma Giri Vipassana International Academy in Igatpuri and Dhamma Khetta Vipassana International Meditation Centre in Hyderabad.

Best time of year: India's climate varies from region to region, so when it's best to visit will depend on where you go. In general, most areas are affected by the summer monsoon which falls between June and September, and baked in intensely hot temperatures from March to June. The north, closer to the Himalayas, is cooler, particularly during January and February.

Silence is one thing, but staying silent for ten days truly allows you to focus on your inner thoughts

What is the longest you have gone without speaking? A few hours? A day? What if that included no writing, making eye contact or communication of any form for ten whole days? This is the Buddhist practice of Vipassana – meaning to 'see things as they really are' – that aims to bring clarity through observation by sitting still for up to ten hours a day.

And what better place to try such a profound experience than the modern birthplace of the practice: southern India. Arriving in one of the main cities, you will be met by a cacophony of noise; the blare of car horns, shouts from traders, the chatter of millions of city dwellers. But enter a Vipassana centre and all that fades away...

Open to people of all faiths and free to all, the ancient meditation technique was rediscovered by the Buddha 2,500 years ago and taught as 'a universal remedy for all ills'. It was passed down from teacher to teacher and popularized in the 1960s by Burmese tutor Satya Narayan Goenka, who set up the first retreat in Hyderabad, southern India, to help teach people how to manage their minds. After all, what good is silence on the outside, if inside your head is full of thoughts and emotions? Our reality is only as clear as our thoughts and speaking is the perfect way to avoid truly registering those patterns.

Waking at 4am, you spend the first three days simply observing the breath (*apana*); in the nostrils, the tip of the nose, the back of the throat. After that, you graduate to long body scans – bringing awareness to any bodily sensations or pain, but not fixating on them. Have an itchy nose? Don't scratch it. Leg gone to sleep? Notice it, but do not readjust your cross-legged position.

The Global Vipassana Pagoda near Gorai, northwest of Mumbai, can seat around 8,000 meditators.

ALSO TRY

Hawaii, USA: Billed as one of the most spiritual places on the planet, this archipelago is well-known for its *mana* (life force). Tap into it and yourself on a weekend or full week-long retreat here organised by Vipassana Hawaii. Look at Big Island, the most sacred of the collective, first.

Myanmar: Visit the birthplace of Satya Narayan Goenka, the teacher who brought new life to the practice of Vipassana in the 1960s. There are a handful of retreats in both the far north and south of the country, but the most established is Dhamma Joti Vipassana Meditation Centre found in Yangon.

South Africa: Vibrant Cape Town seems an odd choice in which to find calm, but Dhamma Patākā, an hour northeast of the capital, is consistently rated one of the best Vipassana retreats in the world.

By reducing the experience purely to the physical we learn that pain or discomfort is only temporary – a sensation that eventually shifts – and that we can respond to difficult emotions, such as anger, guilt or shame in the same way. If we don't get entangled with these feelings, don't react immediately and, instead, sit with them a while, they burn off – like a lit match that sizzles down to smoke. The practice helps us realise our reality varies according to the mind's perception. And that if we can master the mind, we have a chance to glimpse the true nature of reality – not just the version clouded by our own preconceptions and judgements.

Naturally, it is incredibly challenging. Participants report that it makes you 'realize how reliant we are on talking – how habitually we use it as a way of releasing stress.' They say no matter how much you are raging to express yourself, the practice of Vipassana is 'much like surgery: you do not leave halfway through.' And, slowly, slowly, sitting in silence will build strength and focus until you meet yourself in a

profound way. Practitioners call it 'self-transformation' – a place of non-delusion and peace – that liberates you from suffering because you are no longer enslaved by your thoughts. Just as we use exercise to train the body, so Vipassana strengthens the mind.

Indeed, many report not wanting to break their vow of silence once the ten-day retreat concludes, recalling: 'When you come out of silence, speaking again feels like breaking a fast. It purifies your speech in the same way fasting purifies the system. No-one wants to come out of it. Silence becomes a beautiful friend.'

Indian spiritual leader Ravi Shankar, also known as Sri Sri, describes it thus: 'The whole of life is smiling outwardly and going into silence is like giving yourself that smile.' It teaches you to be alone in a joyful way.

Dhamma Giri in Igatpuri runs residential Vipassana retreats.

Find creativity in the darkness of a Finnish winter

ARTELES CREATIVITY CENTER, FINLAND

Fancy holing up in a cabin in the woods to work on your 'big idea'?

Arteles, two-and-a-half hours north of Helsinki in western Finland, is a residential space that brings together artists and professionals and immerses them in pure nature so they can focus on their creative endeavours. The centre runs four retreats a year to: 'provide freedom for creativity and the courage to dream and to see things from new perspectives.'

Seven kilometres (four miles) from the nearest village, the residency is surrounded by fresh forests of spruce and pine, verdant fields grazed by sheep, and lakes clean enough to swim in. In Finland, they practice 'Everyman's Rights', meaning anyone is free to roam wherever they like, including private land. So in summer, when the sun barely sleeps, you can wander through landscapes ripe with raspberries, cranberries and bilberries, the air scented with wild herbs; through forests home to deer, lynx, moose and even rarely seen bears and wolves.

However, Arteles also runs a special Silence Awareness Existence retreat in the dead of winter. From January to March, daylight barely breaks. The sky only turns a soft lavender before fading back to inky blackness streaked through with stars, and when you're perpetually cocooned in a half-light or darkness creativity takes root and blooms. The milky monotone landscape and the deep snow create a muffled silence ripe for deep artistic work or research – but don't worry, there's no pressure to produce concrete results.

Welcoming between 12 and 14 residents at a time, for a residency lasting one or two months, guests are split between two lodgings, including a beautiful 1902 timber house, with private bedrooms and a shared bathroom. On hand for all manner of creative endeavours is a plethora of equipment, including a photography studio, sewing machines, telescopes, paper and paints, acoustic guitars, keyboards and much more besides.

How to do it: Creatives must be aged 23 or older and need to apply a few months in advance. Tampere-Pirkkala is the nearest airport and has flights offered by SAS, Finnair, Ryanair, airBaltic and some charter companies. Alternatively, you can fly to Finland's capital, Helsinki, and take the 3-hour bus or train journey to Tampere. The Arteles centre will collect you from Tampere.

Best time of year: The Silence Awareness Existence retreat runs from January to March.

The snow-dappled forests surrounding Arteles are the ideal place to seek creative inspiration.

To further fuel guests' ability to concentrate, the retreat incorporates two silent days per week, switches off the Wi-Fi on designated days and offers meditation sessions morning and evening. Everything is designed as a bubble to shield you from outside stresses and pressures leaving you free for personal growth and mindfulness. Projects that people have worked on here are varied: from sculptures made of Finnish wool and plans for a play about sex robots, to flowers preserved in ice and soundscape poetry. It's all about embracing the organic flow of creativity that nature inspires in you. Brazilian journalist, Julia Anadam, writes: 'Arteles is a magical place. After a few days (especially without the internet), you go to the forest and you start to hear the words of the wind.'

LEFT *A glimpse of the lake. Come summer it's warm enough to swim in.*

ALSO TRY

Fordypningsrommet, Norway: The northernmost artist's retreat in the world, this stunning collection of stilted modernist timber-clad boxes overlooks the islands of the Fleinvær archipelago and the evocative Norwegian Sea within the Arctic Circle. Only 12 creatives are hosted at any one time and they have a studio, sauna, bathhouse and unlimited nature to kick-start their imagination. Professional artists can apply for free stays, but amateurs are also welcome.

Villa Lena, Tuscany, Italy: A rose-coloured 19th-century neo-Renaissance villa perched above the sloping folds of Tuscan olive groves. In exchange for giving talks and holding workshops, writers, musicians and painters can stay for two months and dine on meals made from the villa's own kitchen garden.

Casa Wabi, Oaxaca, Mexico: Professional artists can apply for a residency at this architect-designed collection of six guesthouses centred around a staggering 'longhouse' of smooth concrete walls and woven palm-leaf roof on the shores of the South Pacific.

But it's not all intense contemplation and creation. There's a traditional 1960s wood-burning sauna to warm up and unwind in, an icy-cold lake for brisk mind-sharpening dips, and some nights the northern lights dance across the sky like blue-and-emerald silk scarves blowing in the frigid wind.

Another participant, Lorraine Hamilton from Glasgow, says: 'I became friends with silence. I was apprehensive about what this new experience might reveal, but I was surprised to find joy in the quiet; a lightness in myself; and a new way of being around others.'

Kayak through calm waters in Poland

GREAT LAKES DISTRICT, POLAND

THE LOWDOWN

How to do it: Olsztyn-Mazury Airport hosts flights from London, Dortmund and Krakow and is 45 minutes from Olsztyn by train. Stara Owczarnia is a recommended *agroturystyka*, or farm stay, run by Joanna and her British husband Paul Easton and their dogs Chester and Louie.

Best time of year: September allows you to avoid the summer crowds (and mosquitoes) while the weather remains reliably warm.

Soulful contemplation doesn't always mean having to sit still

Picture slipping a kayak into a glass-clear river while the early morning mist hangs low across the fields like a giant gossamer spider web. Juvenile perch and larger pike weave through reeds that wave like long tresses of hair in the gentle current. Birds call from the shoreline and, rounding a bend, the guttural growl of a stag echoes from the woods. This is the experience of kayaking on the Krutynia – the longest river of Poland's Great Lakes District.

Straddling the two *voivodeships* (provinces) of Warmia and Mazury – from Węgorzewo in the north to Pisz and Ruciane-Nida in the south – and three hours north of the capital Warsaw, this area has 2,000 lakes and very few visitors. A finalist for the New Seven Wonders of Nature list in 2011, it forms Europe's most-extensive waterway and is heaven for kayakers.

Surrounding it are sun-dappled forests of hornbeam, pine and oak, bursting with berries and mushrooms and home to wild boar, deer, wolves, badgers and red squirrels. If you stand still, silence descends. A silence so profound it soaks into your bones and unlocks all that is clenched inside you. Locals even speak of people feeling 'high' here because there's so much fresh air thanks to so few cars and so many trees.

At the region's centre is the garden town of Olszytn. Bordered by forest and carved in half by the Łyna River, its café-lined cobbled streets congregate around an ancient town hall and a 14th-century castle. While, a short drive east, on the outskirts of Gierłoż, is Wilczy Szaniec (Wolf's Lair) – one of Adolf Hitler's secret military headquarters that lives in infamy as the site where Claus von Stauffenberg, an officer in the German Resistance, failed to assassinate Hitler on 20 July 1944 during the *Valkyrie* operation. Hidden among a swathe of oaks, it is couched in an altogether more eerie silence.

Poland's Great Lake District.

Many people may still have Poland pegged as a grey communist country characterized by donkey-pulled carts and dreary food, but that's not the case. The region is dotted with cosy family-run restaurants, such as Słowiczówka in Utka, serving both typical and inventive Masurian cooking which, as you'd expect, features plenty of fish.

Polish locals flock to the region in summer, and at weekends the river is bustling with boats. Holiday-makers build log rafts and set up floating BBQs in the middle of the river to roast sausages and drink wine. Better to visit when the hot days of July and August have passed, and everyone has returned to work. Then, when the sun is slinking towards the horizon, slide your kayak into the river and let the lazy current pull you along. Notice the pearlescent glimmer of clam shells on the clean bottom and watch swans and their cygnets plumb the shallows. At times, you may suspect you've gone deaf it's so quiet here, with only the faintest ripple of your oar splitting the placid water and wide blue sky.

St James Cathedral in Olszytn, the unofficial capital of Poland's Great Lakes District.

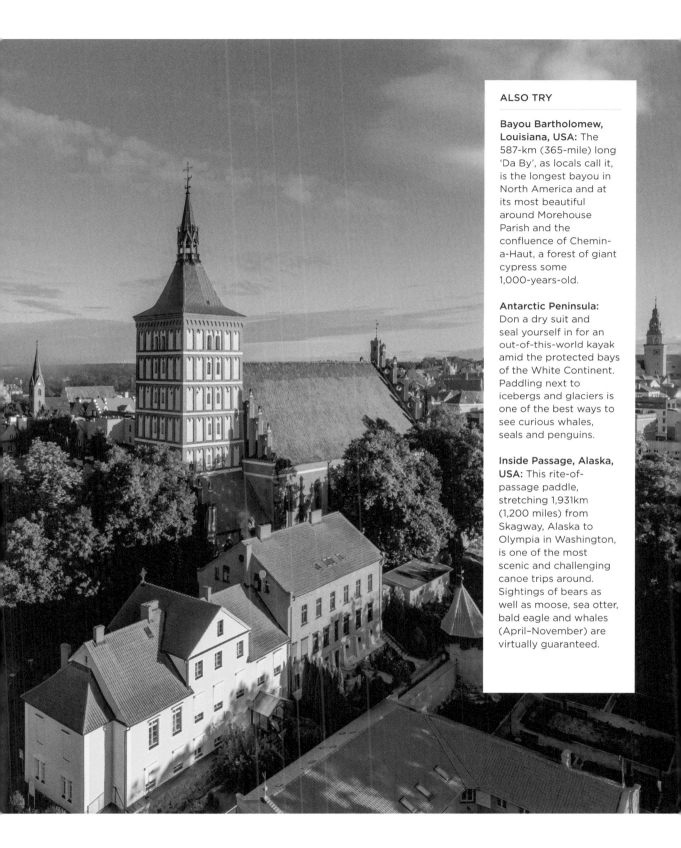

ALSO TRY

Bayou Bartholomew, Louisiana, USA: The 587-km (365-mile) long 'Da By', as locals call it, is the longest bayou in North America and at its most beautiful around Morehouse Parish and the confluence of Chemin-a-Haut, a forest of giant cypress some 1,000-years-old.

Antarctic Peninsula: Don a dry suit and seal yourself in for an out-of-this-world kayak amid the protected bays of the White Continent. Paddling next to icebergs and glaciers is one of the best ways to see curious whales, seals and penguins.

Inside Passage, Alaska, USA: This rite-of-passage paddle, stretching 1,931km (1,200 miles) from Skagway, Alaska to Olympia in Washington, is one of the most scenic and challenging canoe trips around. Sightings of bears as well as moose, sea otter, bald eagle and whales (April–November) are virtually guaranteed.

SILENT SPAS AND WELLNESS RETREATS

'All of humanity's problems stem from man's inability to sit quietly in a room alone.'

BLAISE PASCAL

Cosy up in rustic seclusion

STILLPOINT LODGE, ALASKA, USA

How to do it:
Anchorage International Airport is the gateway to Alaska. Connecting flights to Homer, located 20km (12 miles) from the lodge, are operated by regional airline Ravn Alaska. From Homer, Stillpoint offers a complimentary transfer via boat. Alternatively, you can rent a car and make the 5-hour drive from Anchorage to Homer. Stillpoint also offers a 1-hour transfer via floatplane direct from Anchorage to the lodge.

Best time of year:
Alaska is best visited from May to September when the weather is milder. The spawning salmon also attract bears (often with cubs May–June) during this period. Be aware that summers (June–July) bring 22 hours of daylight, so you might want to pack an eyemask to help with sleep.

The big wide open spaces of Alaska are perfect for finding peace

It's the great, big, broad land 'way up yonder,
It's the forests where silence has lease;
It's the beauty that thrills me with wonder,
It's the stillness that fills me with peace.
Robert Service

Alaska's tooth-and-claw wilderness has always attracted those seeking silence. It is an untamed state that calls to adventurers and free spirits looking to live on the precipice of safe. Here everything is bigger: the forests, the vegetables, the bears, the bugs. And best of all it is home to hardly anyone. In fact, if Manhattan had the same population density as Alaska only 16 people would live here.

One lodge in particular calls for you to contemplate this wildness 'without and within'. Set amid a raw unspoilt theatre of nature, on the fringes of the forested Kachemak Bay State Park, and just across the bay from Homer, sits the rustic Stillpoint Lodge. No roads lead here, the local post office floats and wildlife easily outnumbers the local community. The clue is in the name: everything here is arranged to amplify the abundance of stillness and serenity the location affords.

Maroon yourself in Alaska's raw nature at Stillpoint Lodge.

Path of Love, Yorkshire, UK: Set amid the rolling Yorkshire Dales, this seven-day spiritually-based personal development workshop is so effective that it relies solely on word-of-mouth referrals. There are no phones, laptops or books allowed and there is no yoga – just a chance to learn how to connect with people more authentically.

Silent Meditation Camp Rishikesh, Uttarakhand, India: In the foothills of northern India's Himalayas, Rishikesh is one of the holiest places in the world for Hindus. Join the many sages and saints who have meditated here on a three-, seven-, fifteen- or twenty-one-day meditation camp staying in mud huts beside the sacred River Ganga.

Kailash International Retreat Centre, Törbel, Switzerland: Perched amid the jaws of the staggeringly beautiful Swiss Alps, this tranquil centre teaches Kadampa (a branch of Buddhism) silent meditation techniques over a long weekend to a week and provides solitary retreats lasting a few months if you so wish.

For those with previous experience of meditation, there is a chance to delve even deeper into solitude with a stay by themselves at the Kuti (Thai for meditation) hut. This off-grid hermitage, set in a patch of private woodland in the grounds of The Barn, is a real step back in time. With no electricity, just candles, and no running water (you can use a shower in The Barn), this snug wattle-and-daub hideaway has a simple single bed on a low wooden frame, camping stove, meditation mat, a separate compost loo and a cosy wood-burning stove. It is no frills, but importantly it is extremely affordable for visitors of limited means. Meals can be prepared by The Barn staff and collected, or you can be completely self-sufficient – don't miss a bottle or two of apple juice pressed from the estate's own orchards, or even its acclaimed hand-made cheese.

If you would to have a few more amenities, the rustic Cabin located near The Barn's organic garden also just sleeps one, but has its own running water, a raised bed, a proper kitchen space with stocked pantry and more homely furnishings – although you will still have to stroll downhill to the compost loo. When staying at both, you are asked to spend one or two hours a day working on the land and then organize your own unguided meditation sessions.

Sharpham Estate offers multiple entry points into silence for single travellers, no matter how new or established your relationship with it is.

OPPOSITE *Vines growing in the Sharpham vineyard.*

ABOVE *Book a Woodland Retreat and you'll sleep in bell tents, eat vegetarian food and wander the woods.*

Let silence lead you to the inner 'you'

THE HERMITAGE, GUATEMALA

Seen from space, Lago de Atitlán spreads across the Guatemalan Highlands like a bird in flight

How to do it: The international gateway to Guatemala is La Aurora airport. From there, it's a 4-hour drive to Lake Atitlán and The Hermitage. Public transport is an option, but a far quicker alternative is to arrange a private taxi for US$100. Public transport involves taking a 45-minute airport shuttle to Antigua and then taking a tourist shuttle to the lake, each costing US$25. However, the last shuttles leaves Antigua at 2pm, so if your flight arrives later than midday, you will need to stay a night in Antigua first. Guatemala offers a three-month visa on arrival.

A deep and ancient caldera encircled by three volcanoes, the waters of Lago de Atitlán are mirror-calm in the morning and frisky as a bag of cats by the afternoon. It's a mystical landscape declared 'the most beautiful lake in the world' by 19th-century German explorer, Alexander von Humboldt, and is Central America's deepest body of water. Rich in birdlife and painted with the pink pop of hibiscus flowers, its shoreline is dotted with cobblestone-street towns – many reachable only by boat – lined with markets selling home-woven rainbow-coloured textile tops and skirts and an abundance of avocados, strawberries, dragon fruit, corn, cucumbers, tomatoes and beans, grown on the surrounding verdant mountain slopes. Mayan culture still predominates and in days gone by illness was not necessarily a physical ailment, but a spiritual one.

Best time of year: Guatemala is called 'the land of eternal spring' due to its perfect tropical temperatures. In general, aim for the dry season between December and May when temperatures hover around 24–27°C (75–80°F) at the elevated Lake Atitlán.

Enter The Hermitage – a family-owned retreat established by Swiss-born Severin Geser and his New Zealand wife Emma – perched on its own lakeside patch of Atitlán a five-minute-walk from San Pablo la Laguna, a Mayan village with around 8,000 inhabitants and no tourism. In the past, Severin spent 14 months as an ordained monk in a Thai monastery, worked as an Ashtanga Yoga teacher in Colombia, and spent two years in and out of extended silent meditation retreats. Meanwhile Emma is trained in the Hindu philosophy of Advaita Vedanta and spent the large part of four years in silence and contemplative retreat.

Together, they've created a non-religious, Wi-Fi-free space for silent and dark retreats spanning anything from a week to over three months. Group retreats are offered, but most guests choose to isolate in private cabins. They offer four with a lounge, fully equipped kitchen, balcony, private garden and a private eco-bathroom with solar shower. The pick of the bunch is the rustic Forest Cabin set apart from the main sections of the centre in a thicket of bamboo with stunning private views of the lake, followed closely by the Swiss Family Robinson-style three-level Tree House with two

Stay at The Hermitage and you'll spend a lot of time in their beautiful meditation hall.

6-m (20-ft) high meditation platforms overlooking the coffee plantation and a separate temple room. There are also three cheaper private rooms and a dormitory fitted with capsule beds all built from natural materials. Groceries can be delivered and prepared in your private equipped kitchen, or vegetarian meals delivered to your door so that you can better maintain a steady practice. Everything is infused with wholesomeness, from the honey harvested by neighbouring beekeepers, to the home-grown coffee and home-brewed kombucha.

Guests have access to a circular meditation hall with arresting floor-to-ceiling views of the lake, a library stocked with spiritual literature, permaculture gardens and the ethereal lakefront white-sand beach and pier.

If you'd like to delve deeper, enter their dark rooms. Choose from the adobe-and-bamboo Buddha Cave positioned at the top of a hill behind a sacred amate tree, or the underground Tara Room made of river stones and crystals. Enter a candle-lit space and when ready blow out the flame. You can stay for a single day or over a month. 'In there, it's just you, your mind and your inner light that shines,' says Emma. 'It offers deep physical rest. With no schedules, phones or responsibilities, the mind can let go. What is hidden can rise up. It's the next level in meditation.'

Severin also offers free astrology readings to retreaters and Emma offers deep-healing massage and counselling. As one of the only foreigner-run businesses in San Pablo, it's also good to know that a percentage of guests' fees go towards sponsoring local children so they can attend school and towards providing food packages for families in need. So, sit back and spend hours observing the ever-steady silhouettes of the volcanoes in the hazy, lazy heat as fishermen in narrow wooden boats glide across the surface of this otherworldly lake.

RIGHT *Relaxing accommodation with lake views.*

OPPOSITE *The Hermitage sits on the shores of Lake Atitlán and its arresting ring of volcanoes.*

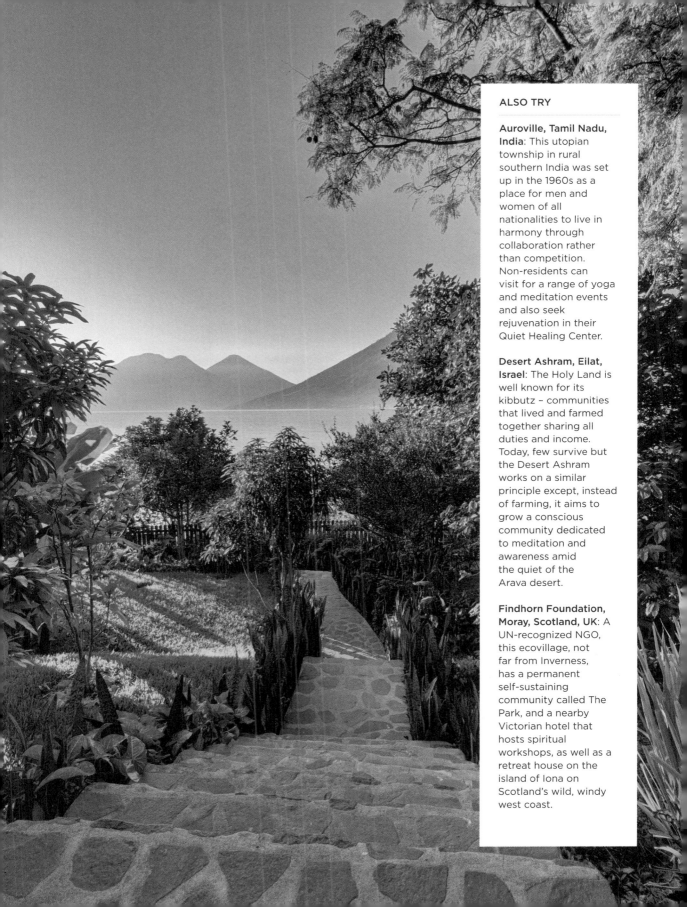

ALSO TRY

Auroville, Tamil Nadu, India: This utopian township in rural southern India was set up in the 1960s as a place for men and women of all nationalities to live in harmony through collaboration rather than competition. Non-residents can visit for a range of yoga and meditation events and also seek rejuvenation in their Quiet Healing Center.

Desert Ashram, Eilat, Israel: The Holy Land is well known for its kibbutz – communities that lived and farmed together sharing all duties and income. Today, few survive but the Desert Ashram works on a similar principle except, instead of farming, it aims to grow a conscious community dedicated to meditation and awareness amid the quiet of the Arava desert.

Findhorn Foundation, Moray, Scotland, UK: A UN-recognized NGO, this ecovillage, not far from Inverness, has a permanent self-sustaining community called The Park, and a nearby Victorian hotel that hosts spiritual workshops, as well as a retreat house on the island of Iona on Scotland's wild, windy west coast.

Fill your lungs with fresh air (while indulging in luxury)

THE ALPINA GSTAAD, GSTAAD, SWITZERLAND

Silence does not always have to mean paired back

Set amid Switzerland's pointy peaks and lush meadows that echo with the tinkle of cowbells, this sumptuous five-star hotel is the first luxury hotel built in Gstaad for a century. It's a member of the Lartisien Grand Luxury Hotels group, which makes it sound rather brash, but the Alpina is a small and discreet 56-room property that is a good option for parents seeking stillness with children in tow.

Declared 'The place to be seen' by *Time* magazine in the 1960s, Gstaad has had cameos in F Scott Fitzgerald's novel *Tender is the Night* and Peter Sellers's *The Return of the Pink Panther*. This small ski-resort town could easily be nicknamed the Aspen of Europe thanks to its popularity with the wealthy and famous: Elizabeth Taylor, Grace Kelly, Roger Moore, Madonna and Prince Charles have all come here to whoosh down the ski slopes and browse the town's main street lined with Louis Vuitton, Hermès, Prada and Cartier stores.

But the Alpina Gstaad is elevated, not ostentatious. Its timber-clad exterior, with window boxes brimming with scarlet geraniums, matches the local Simmentaler architectural style and the decor has Swiss accents: from rugs woven from Saanenland goat hair and lights that resemble cowbells, to Alpine-mined quartz for the beer taps, as well as an extensive private art collection featuring a neon sign by Tracey Emin.

The rooms are rustic with muted linens and roaring fires, and they range from the one-bedroom Deluxe to the three-bedroom Panorama Suite with its own private spa featuring a sauna, hammam and outdoor Jacuzzi.

How to do it: Start your journey to The Alpina Gstaad slowly by taking the train from Geneva's central railway station, Gare Cornavin, to Montreux and then book a seat aboard the iconic GoldenPass Montreux-Oberland Bernois (MOB) railway line to Gstaad. Alternatively, the nearest international airport is Bern-Belp Airport and it's located 1 hour and 20 minutes away by car, or 2.5 hours away by train. If you're flying into Zurich Airport the drive will take 3 hours; the train 3 hours and 30 minutes.

Best time of year: The Alpina Gstaad has a winter season (mid-December to mid-March) and summer season (mid-June to mid-September). Winter brings muffled silence and an ethereal world of white; summer brings vibrant wildflower meadows.

Nestled amid the trees, the Alpina Gstaad is a movie star in her own right.

ALSO TRY

Bagni Vecchi, Lombardy, Italy:
Roman-scholar Pliny the Elder and Renaissance-man Leonardo da Vinci have both soaked in the thermal waters of this historic spa in the heart of the Italian Alps. Don't miss the panoramic pool with mountain vistas and the San Martino steam cave, which leads to one of the thousand-year-old springs. Stay at the nearby five-star Grand Hotel Bagni Nuovi that could easily be mistaken as the location of Wes Anderson's *The Grand Budapest Hotel* movie thanks to its candy-pink Art-Nouveau façade.

Aqua Dome, Tirol, Austria: 'Voices down and clothes off' is the rule when enjoying the earth, hay and herb-scented saunas that form part of this vast, high-design spa hotel which sits at the base of a valley in the Ötztal Alps. Grown-ups can soak away their stress in the giant Jacuzzis, and for the little ones there's the child-focused Alpen Arche Noah.

Secret Lagoon, Flúðir, Iceland: Far better than Iceland's famous Blue Lagoon is the rural and rugged Secret Lagoon, an hour and a half east of the capital Reykjavic. Over a century old, word of its volcanic-heated pool has spread far, but it remains relatively uncrowded and there's the added chance of seeing the northern lights in winter.

Waiting to smooth out every stressed muscle in your body is the Six Senses Spa – the only one of its kind in Switzerland. This sanctuary of Zen offers inventive treatments that range from Tibetan moxibustion (the burning of moxa wool above specific points on the body to unblock energy channels), to Kundalini massages to restore the body's natural biorhythms, to facials of green caviar and gold, and body scrubs using salt crystals extracted from glaciers in the Swiss Alps. Not to mention a colour-therapy room and a healing grotto built from blocks of pink-Himalayan salt.

Once your mind and body are feeling mellow, you can indulge in some gastronomic therapy. Balance out a healthy breakfast of egg-white omelette, fresh-pressed vegetable juice and quinoa cereal with a belt-busting fondue or raclette at the Swiss Stübli restaurant come nightfall, or for a more refined evening, head to the Michelin-starred Sommet with a menu designed around the chef's world travels.

While mum and dad are indulging in all this, children can try salt-dough play and painting at the Tree House Club or book the private on-site cinema. While outdoors, families can hike, bike, paraglide, ice skate (in winter), take a family hot-air balloon ride, or learn about the little world of bees from the hotel's resident beekeeper. All these activities are a reminder that, come winter or summer, this is a place to immerse yourself in nature – a place to stretch the legs and mind. And when looking for meditative calm where better place to start than a country renowned for its pacifist stance and staying neutral during conflicts?

OPPOSITE *Wash away your stress at the Alpina Gstaad's heated outdoor pool.*

BELOW *One of the many peaceful spaces at Alpina Gstaad.*

Feed mind, body and soul at an off-grid retreat

SILENT RETREAT, BALI

THE LOWDOWN

How to do it: Bali has one international airport, Ngurah Rai, in the south of the island. Bali Silent Retreat is located a 2 hour-drive north of the airport. The centre can arrange a transfer if booked at least 24 hours in advance, or you can hire a taxi. If you're feeling flush, a 20-minute helicopter transfer is also available with Air Bali.

Best time of year: Aim for the dry season that falls between April and September; but if rain doesn't bother you, January and February see far fewer visitors. Temperatures average between 26–30°C (79–86°F) year-round.

Relax in a place where every element exists to feed your physical and spiritual health

Sometimes we want to explore silence without the intensity of complete isolation (see page 174) or a full Vipassana meditation (see page 148). For those times, there is the Silent Retreat in Bali. Set amid the UNESCO-listed rice terraces of Tabanan, two and a half hours north of the capital, Denpasar, this off-grid eco-sustainable sanctuary is a place to simply *be*.

Here you are encouraged to practise the art of nothing. So sit beneath the trickling streams of the water meditation area and let them wash away the stress; pace the crystal-surrounded labyrinth; absorb the plant power of the medicine garden; walk the jungle path; release deep emotions and memories on the solitary Crying Bench; sleep beneath the sky on the stargazing beds; travel the rice paddy path; or laze in a hammock with a library book in hand.

Days follow a loose pattern of being woken at sunrise with fresh ginger tea brought to your room, gathering beneath the open-air octagonal *bale* (tent) for morning meditation and a class of gentle hatha yoga. You'll listen to the birds in the surrounding trees, the croak of frogs and feel the cool morning air whisper on your skin. By late morning, you'll be soaking in the rock-clad pools of the local hot springs and each night, after sunset, you'll gather around a fire where blank paper waits for you to write or journal.

This is a truly green property with zero carbon footprint. Showers and lights are solar powered, no pesticides are used to grow the food, and nothing that cannot be composted or reused is allowed onto the property – so any plastics or batteries guests bring in must be taken away with them and disposed of in their own country.

The many-tiered Jatiluwih Rice Terraces are a UNESCO World Heritage Site.

DAY OF SILENCE

Other cultures celebrate New Year's Eve with raucous parties, but the predominantly Hindu island of Bali does it differently. Their New Year falls in March and they celebrate with a six-day festival punctuated in the middle with an official 'Day of Silence' called *Nyepi*, where the entire island shuts down for the day. This nearly 2,000-year-old ritual, involving silence, fasting and meditation, is an official holiday for self-reflection, to strengthen the connection to God and evaluate personal values such as love, patience and kindness.

As Bali's most sacred holiday, Hindus have the day off work and are forbidden from other distractions such as TV, radio or internet, travelling, talking and eating. Homeowners close their curtains, hotels board up their windows and no lights or candles are lit. Even the international airport closes. Travellers and non-Hindus must observe the rules too and stay inside their hotels.

Accommodation is a mixture of very simple single rooms or rustic, grass-roofed bungalows made of recycled wood which overlook the rice fields and sacred Mount Batu Karu. All feature a private bathroom with an open-air hot shower and are free of Wi-Fi and other electronic distractions.

Meals – three vegetarian buffets daily – are prepared from the on-site organic gardens and feature dishes such as salad with foraged wild herbs, grated root vegetables and sprouts, homemade duck-egg noodles with spinach and coconut sauce, young papaya salad or sorbet made of beetroot and turmeric. The chef's aim is to free you from sugar, alcohol and meat cravings and restore your body to a healthful state. Guests are encouraged to eat mindfully, by chewing slowly and savouring each bite.

The retreat's ethos is not shaped by any religion, dogma or guru. Its only aim is to restore wholeness. So, if the need to speak becomes overwhelming, there are chat zones where you can converse with other guests. And if your mind needs a little distraction, you can join workshops about medicinal plants, listen to the gentle percussive local *gamelan* music featuring the bamboo flute, or immerse yourself in a sound bath session with singing brass bowls.

Perhaps the most potent activity is the *agnihotra*, a healing fire ceremony performed at each new and full moon. Guests are invited to write down any unwanted feelings they wish to symbolically release and then take turns tossing the paper into the flames. Originally an Ayurvedic practice, it is a powerful way of purifying the self and a fitting end to a retreat-stay that burns away any emotional baggage you may be bearing.

TOP *The lush greenery surrounding The Silent Retreat immediately calms the soul.*

BOTTOM *Bali is a hugely spiritual island where locals make daily offerings to their Hindu gods.*

Take succour in everyday tasks

PLUM VILLAGE, DORDOGNE, FRANCE

THE LOWDOWN

How to do it: The nearest international airport is Bordeaux–Mérignac. From there, take the 45-minute shuttle to Bordeaux St-Jean train station where you can catch connections to Sainte Foy la Grande, the station closest to Plum Village, which can arrange a pick-up/drop off. Alternatively, a taxi will cost €40–60. Another option is carpooling for the drive from Paris or Bordeaux. All retreats should be booked well in advance due to their popularity.

Best time of year: Plum Village run retreats throughout the year, check online (see page 249) for availability.

'Meditation is not to escape from society, but to come back to ourselves and see what is going on.'

Thích Nhất Hạnh

Think of a monastery and your mind probably conjures images of gilded buildings clinging to cliff ledges, or serene temples buried deep in the jungle. You wouldn't think to find one at a former farm in the French countryside, an hour and a half's drive east of Bordeaux. But Plum Village is just that; Europe's largest Buddhist monastery spread over four different hamlets and founded by one of the most influential spiritual leaders of our time.

Situated in the commune of Thénac, it was established in the 1980s by Nobel Peace Prize-nominated Buddhist monk Thích Nhất Hạnh (see page 187). He went on to establish 11 other monasteries worldwide, but Plum Village was the very first and today more than 200 monks and nuns reside in the community.

Buddhism is practised by roughly 500 million people worldwide. Its main tenet is that all suffering is a result of craving and attachment and one of its most well-known techniques to combat this is meditation. At Plum Village they practise Engaged Buddhism; this involves actively seeking ways to apply Buddhist teachings to contemporary situations, by weaving mindfulness and periods of silence into daily activities whether it's walking, eating or working. Getting involved in daily chores – from preparing meals and washing dishes, to cleaning toilets – is also part of the practice.

How many of us rush from one task to another during our busy lives without really paying any attention? How often do we drive somewhere without remembering the journey, or spend time with someone but remember little of the conversation? This level of unconsciousness does us a disservice and stops us from experiencing life on a deeper level. Plum Village retreats aim to break this cycle and teach the art of mindful living.

Thích Nhất Hạnh leading guests through the grounds of Plum Village many years prior to his passing.

Described as, 'a home away from home,' it offers spring and autumn retreats that invite guests to stay for one or two weeks, as well as special themed retreats on health, education or ecology. Alternatively, if you're looking to make a greater commitment, it runs an annual month-long summer retreat, or three-month-long winter retreat allowing you to completely immerse yourself for 90 consecutive days and deepen your practice. And if you're in need of a complete overhaul, there are opportunities to stay from six months to a year as well. All the options include regular talks on self-acceptance, happiness and healing. Afterwards, attendees have reported a diminishment in both their anxiety or depression and a deep-rooted sense of wellbeing.

People of all religious backgrounds (as well as sexual orientation and gender identity) are welcome, and participants are asked to refrain from sex, smoking and consumption of alcohol or drugs while on site. Plum Village follows a vegan diet, with meals prepared from the organic communal garden, and any non-vegan foods are prohibited. Accommodation is mostly communal dormitories.

This isn't really a holiday, but rather a peaceful bootcamp for the mind. A nourishing cocoon that offers structured ways to explore silence and rediscover the meaning of *sangha* (community), which for many of us has shrunk or become fragmented. A reminder that meditation isn't just for monks, but rather a tool we can all employ for a daily dose of serenity.

Guests listening to Buddhist teachings beneath the trees, Plum Village, France.

WHO WAS THÍCH NHẤT HẠNH?

Born in Vietnam in 1926, Thích Nhất Hạnh (pronounced 'Tik N'yat Hawn') became a Buddhist monk aged 16. When the Vietnam War hit, instead of solely meditating on peace he chose to actively help those suffering. In 1965 he wrote a letter to Dr Martin Luther King urging him to denounce the war. They met a year later and King – who called Nhất Hạnh 'an apostle of peace' – nominated the monk for the Nobel Peace Prize. Nhất Hạnh's calls for an end to the war resulted in a 39-year exile from Vietnam. He went on to teach at both Princeton and Columbia Universities in the USA, as well as the Sorbonne in Paris and, shortly after, founded the Sweet Potato community on the outskirts of the French capital. Its name was a nod to solidarity with Vietnam's poorest, who eat the potatoes when they can't afford rice. In 1982, the community moved to the larger site of Plum Village in the Dordogne and Nhất Hạnh lived there until 2018 when ill health led him back home to Vietnam. He died in 2022 in the same temple he was ordained in aged 16.

Expand your mind

ESALEN INSTITUTE, CALIFORNIA, USA

How to do it: Esalen
offers two options: stays
of five days and four
nights or three days and
two nights. Most
travellers fly into San
Francisco International
Airport and either rent
a car and drive the
3 hours to Big Sur, or
catch a connecting
flight to Monterey
Regional Airport, which
is a 75-minute drive or
bus ride from Big Sur.
Be aware the Monterey–
Salinas Transit bus route
only runs on weekends
in the winter, and drive
times can be severely
affected by summer
holiday and weekend
traffic.

Best time of year: Big
Sur's peak season runs
from April to October
and its beauty attracts
big crowds, so it's best
to visit between
September and
November for less
traffic and less coastal
fog. February tends to
be the wettest month.

Esalen isn't a spa retreat; it's a centre that invites a whole new way of being and thinking

Perched between the foaming rollers of the Pacific Ocean and the redwood-clad hills of Pfeiffer State Park, 20km (12 miles) south of Big Sur in California, Esalen sits on the longest scenic stretch of undeveloped coastline in the USA.

It was established in the 1960s as a holistic education centre 'for exploring and realizing human potential through experience, education and research to work towards a more just, creative and sustainable world by offering spiritual and social transformation programs and workshops.'

Since its very beginning, a litany of greats have worked, taught and lived here, including: writers Henry Miller, Aldous Huxley and Joseph Campbell – even a young Hunter S Thompson, who worked as a security guard; folk singer Joan Baez; psychiatrist Fritz Perls, founder of Gestalt therapy; and Abraham Maslow of Maslow's Hierarchy of Needs.

Today, workshops run the gamut from learning the secret of great relationships and tantra to unlocking creativity and immersive dance. Daily activities include yoga, breathwork and journaling sessions, as well as soaking in the mineral hot springs (clothing optional) overlooking the rocky shoreline, which is visited by sea otters and whales.

View of Esalen and the Big Sur coastline, California, USA.

Food will also play a major role during your stay. You'll be eating organic fare harvested less than 400 paces away on the on-site farm and guests are encouraged to connect with the land by joining mindful harvesting of the fruits, herbs and heirloom vegetables. And because this is Esalen, you'll perhaps find yourself dunking homemade bread into a cauliflower coconut curry and debating bread's history and symbolic uses – from the braided Jewish *challah* being a slice of heaven, to Turkey where two loaves are paid for at the bakery but one left as an act of kindness for a stranger who cannot afford to buy their own. The centre exists to get you to think more deeply about the customs and traditions we often take for granted and whether there are better, kinder, more effective ways of being.

Meanwhile, accommodation ranges from a sleeping bag on the floor of the meeting room (for those on a budget), to private houses boasting ocean views, an outdoor clawfoot tub and a cosy wood-burning stove. All are, purposely, without television, alarm clock, mobile phone reception or internet access.

Other facilities include a pool, meditation hut, a spa offering bespoke massages, and a turquoise art barn stocked with paper, paint, brushes, clay and other mediums to create or experiment as you like. There's also an artist-in-residence who can offer guidance or lessons, too.

One of the most powerful elements about staying at Esalen is being surrounded by the silent shaping ways of water: whether that's drinking from the freshwater spring, immersing yourself in the natural hot thermals – which originally put Big Sur on the map – or staring out at the frisky and vast Pacific Ocean. All of them evoke an expansive silence in the soul.

And you'll need to access that silence in order to let go of entrenched ideas about who you are, how the world works and your place in it – to really figure out what it means to be human. Esalen staff freely admit it's a challenge that takes energy, time and space, but happily Esalen provides just that amid a setting of raw natural beauty. As one teacher said: 'They come to meditate, they come to dance, they come to connect. To create, to question, to reflect. To find clarity. And they leave changed, and ready to change the world.'

Meals at Esalen are prepared using ingredients from the retreat's own organic garden.

A NEW WAY OF THINKING

Esalen was founded in 1962 by Stanford graduates Michael Murphy and Dick Price. While living in San Francisco in the 1950s, Price rented a room at the new American Academy of Asian Studies, set up by British philosopher Alan Watts, and counted the Beat Generation poets Jack Kerouac and Allen Ginsberg among his friends.

During this time, Price had a manic episode. His parents had him committed to a mental asylum against his will and, for a year, he was subjected to electroconvulsive therapy (ECT) and potent tranquilizers.

On his release, he felt fundamental mistakes had been made about his illness: 'the mistake was supposing that the healing process was the disease, rather than the process whereby the disease is healed.'

Wanting to find alternative methods of healing, he set up Esalen with Murphy whose family owned the Big Sur property. Meanwhile, Murphy pioneered Esalen's social projects, which included a Soviet-American exchange programme that, in 1990, initiated Boris Yeltsin's first trip to the USA and became a pivotal trip in the ending of the Cold War. Quite an accomplishment for the two men.

Step away from daily life

KAUSAY, SPAIN

How to do it: The nearest airports are Valencia or Alicante or you can catch the train to the nearest station Xativa, which is a 2–3 hours drive away. Kausay can arrange pick-ups from all these locations. Stays are donation based.

Best time of year: Summers in Spain can be hot, with the mercury often pushing 30°C (90°F). For this reason, travellers find the spring months of April and May and autumn months of September and October to be more pleasant – with sunny, warm days free of stifling heat.

Whether you go for a short-break or choose to live off-grid for a little longer, the benefits will seep into your soul

Who of us hasn't yearned for a life free from bills and the 9-to-5 grind; to have a routine governed by daylight and cockerels, instead of clocks; and perhaps to live as part of a close-knit community where connections are unfractured by constant phone and screen use? Two Dutch couples, Ellen and Jeroen and Inge and Brother, and their children, had this yearning, and so they set up Kausay – an off-grid community in Valencia, eastern Spain.

Hidden in a valley outside of mobile-network reach and surrounded by olive groves, orange groves and fields of grazing horses, Kausay is a collection of Mongolian yurts with an organic garden, steeped in quiet and the sweet scent of pine and wild herbs. Kausay is an Incan word meaning 'Life Force' and this is what the families try to restore to their guests in a landscape barely changed since Roman times.

On this land, Ellen – who is trained in mindfulness-based stress reduction and has attended Vipassana (the Buddhist practice of silent meditation) retreats for over 20 years – guides five-day silent retreats. These follow a relaxed schedule beginning with morning yoga and include *yatra* (silent meditative walks), singing circles and meditative dance, interspersed with talks on the senses and *metta* (the Buddhist ideal of loving kindness). No previous experience of meditation is required.

If sitting still sounds frustrating, then Ellen also hosts five-day walking retreats because she believes the very act of placing one foot in front of the other calms the mind and keeps you focused on the present, reconnecting you with your body and the Earth.

The light in Spain has a special sparkle, pay attention to it.

ALSO TRY

Shambala Gatherings, Skinnskatteberg, Sweden: This homely lakeside community of artists and yogis opens its doors to top international yoga and spiritual teachers running retreats. On the fringes of the elk-filled forests of Bergslagen and with a floating wood sauna, it's undoubtedly beautiful in summer but best visited in the snow-muffled silence of winter.

New Life, Serra Da Estrela, Portugal: If you're suffering from burnout, anxiety, depression or loneliness this wellness retreat offers a holistic blend of meditation and yoga combined with counselling and life-coaching in a community setting in order to cultivate a sense of belonging. All set amid the mountains of central Portugal.

Joali Being, Bodufushi, Maldives: A holiday to the Maldives offers peace and quiet anyway, but this transformational luxury resort goes above and beyond to help you reconnect, 'to one's self, one another, and one's environment', with an individually tailored mind and body programme created by Oxford- and Harvard-trained doctors.

The centre also offers very affordable week-long family retreats, too. Mornings are spent separately: kids (aged four and over) are entertained by Jeroen (a former social worker) leading them on adventures in nature, such as harvesting vegetables or making music, while parents practise yoga, or meditation, or sit in periods of silence. The afternoons are for family time, such as swimming in the local waterfall or going for ice cream in the village. Come nightfall, parents can take turns looking after the children while their partner takes part in a women's or men's sharing circle beneath the stars.

Families, couples or individuals who'd like to stay longer can apply for a volunteering role and work in the garden in exchange for food and board. Although similar to the concept of 'Wwoofing' (World Wide Opportunities on Organic Farms), Kausay differs in that it's not strict about the number of hours you are expected to work each day, but rather agrees them based on an understanding between the individual and the collective need of the community and, of course, the season.

Outside of this work, you can hike through the valley, bathe in the *fuente* (natural hot springs), take horse-riding lessons, or just laze in a hammock with a good book. But above all, the lesson here is learning how to enjoy community living in the company of two families and a mix of short- and long-term volunteers. To spend quiet days beneath the sun, with your hands in the soil and, at the end of them, sit down to a meal prepared with food you've grown and gathered together, and swap ideas instead of gossip, or just sit in collective silence listening to the wind, or far-off whinny of horses.

Spending time immersed in the land is a key activity at off-grid community Kausay.

Restore intention to life at a women-only retreat

LAGO D'ORTA, ITALY

How to do it: The closest airport is Milan Malpensa. The Mandali Retreat Center arranges guests into groups to share private van transfers for the 1-hour drive. Mama Medicine runs her Italy retreat annually in July.

Best time of year: Italy is *bellissima* all year around. The gelato-scented summers are hot and attract big crowds, so best to visit in spring (March–May) or autumn (September–October) when days are relatively warm and the holidaymakers have dispersed.

Where better to find renewed purpose and energy than on the shores of this beautiful lake?

Spread between the last vestiges of the Dolomites and Alps, northern Italy is a heart-melting mix of medieval towns characterized by clusters of terracotta-tiled roofs, summery yellow, orange and white façades and the occasional ancient stone bell-tower. A hub of culture, the region is famed for its vineyard-clad hills and many lakes. One, however, flies under the radar. The Milanese call it La Cenerentola (Cinderella), because so many tourists overlook it in favour of the more famous lakes of Como and neighbouring Maggiore.

Lago d'Orta has a quality unlike any other. A smile of water that morphs from slate black to brilliant blue and is punctuated by Isola San Giulio, an island less than 300m (985ft) long and dominated by a Benedictine monastery and medieval basilica. Its beauty has attracted some distinguished visitors, from Friedrich Nietzsche and Lord Byron to Robert Browning and Honoré de Balzac. Novelist Edward Docx, who also spent time writing here, describes the lake as having, 'a mysterious, ethereal, almost supernatural quality. There is something for the soul there as well as for the eye. Sometimes a preternatural stillness seems to rise from the deep...The light changes by the hour. Look out in the morning and there's a medieval mist; by noon, the lake is as clear as the Enlightenment; then, by five, a brooding romanticism has descended. You never want to leave.'

Perched on a hilltop overlooking this beguiling lake is Mandali, a non-profit luxury-boutique-hotel-meets-retreat centre designed to help guests disconnect from the pressures of daily life, switch off from technology, and take time to reflect and reset.

A chic oasis decked out in earthy tones of cream, olive green and beige, it has a temple, library and terrace with panoramic views of the lake. Rooms feature stone floors, wooden beams, organic linens and range from stylish dormitories to premium rooms with luxurious freestanding copper baths. Food is high-quality vegetarian buffets. And here there is no spa, but rather a body-care centre with a sleek swimming pool, treatment room, hot tub and sauna.

Deborah Hanekamp – aka Mama Medicine – runs retreats for women to help them reconnect with their sense of self.

Mandali runs its own three- to seven-day retreats, but also hosts other teachers. One of them is Deborah Hanekamp, aka Mama Medicine. Raised as an evangelical northern Baptist in New England, USA, she later left formal religion and travelled to Thailand and the Peruvian Amazon to study yoga, reiki, healing songs and plant medicine with Mestizo shamans. Decades on, and she is highly praised for her non-dogmatic approach to holistic healing.

Each year in July she hosts a week-long retreat designed, 'to return our sense of self that has been wounded, lost or stuck, to the power, purpose and grace of who we really are. To heal the past and restore intention to life.' To do this, she employs crystals, herbs, yoga, meditation, dance, ceremonies at sunrise and sunset, medicine readings of auras – and, of course, periods of silence. It's a women-only programme that, rather uniquely, supports mothers by providing childcare while participants are in session and welcomes partners to stay (although they cannot participate if male).

Hanekamp says: 'I'm not here to fix you because you are not broken. I can only help to encourage your patience, presence and perseverance as you find your way home to yourself. I think we are all inherently spiritual in our own unique way and maybe what we are seeking is the love that connects us all and is ever present within each one of us.'

It's not a message that lands with everyone, but sometimes quiet comes in new and unusual forms and for those seeking answers, they might be found on that hilltop in northern Italy.

Aerial view of The Mandali
Retreat Centre and Lago d'Orta.

ALSO TRY

Dunton Hot Springs, Colorado, USA: A revived 1800s ghost town comprised of hand-hewn log cabins and a traditional saloon that will thrill children, this intimate resort is nestled deep in the San Juan Mountains of the Colorado Rockies. Guests come for the outdoor activities and natural hot springs that are offered in a variety of styles – try the restored 19th-century bathhouse – followed by meditation and yoga sessions.

Schloss Elmau, Bavaria, Germany: Seated at the foot of the snow-dusted Bavarian Alps and their wildflower summer meadows, this former castle has an illustrious history. Kids can kick back at the hotel's original spa with age-appropriate treatments, while adults are directed to the nearby retreat with three spas, a yoga pavilion and treatments that'll have you yodelling with delight.

MarBella, Corfu, Greece: This large family-friendly five-star resort hotel overlooking the Ionian Sea allows for peaceful-connection time with mother-and-daughter/father-and-son spa treatments using organic products.

URBAN OASES

'Now I shall be silent and let the silence divide
that which is true from that which lies.'

RUMI

Sit in a church beneath the open sky

ST DUNSTAN IN THE EAST, LONDON, UK

THE LOWDOWN

How to do it: London is served by Heathrow, Gatwick and London City Airports and the Eurostar rail service from mainland Europe. The nearest underground station to St Dunstan is Monument or Tower Hill. The garden is open daily from 8am to 7pm except on Christmas Day, Boxing Day and New Year's Day. Admission is free.

Best time of year: The garden is quietest on weekdays (avoid lunchtimes) and particularly leafy from late spring to summer. However it holds a special magic in winter if London is blessed with snow.

Finding peace in a city centre is a special kind of magic

Sometimes it can feel as if every nook of London is permeated by noise: by the screech of trains on un-oiled tracks, by the honk of red-bus or black-cab horns, and by the yells of street-side newspaper hawkers. The very buildings themselves seem to hum with the life of the workers that busy themselves within. And people; everywhere people.

But there are pockets of quiet if you know where to look, and one of them is St Dunstan in the East. Halfway between the major tourist attractions of the Tower of London and London Bridge, and set a few streets back from the milk-chocolate-coloured River Thames, this listed church-ruin is now a secret garden where greenery climbs the historic walls, and benches and a trickling fountain offer a cocoon of calm amid the city chaos.

St Dunstan was a 10th-century monk who rose to become the Archbishop of Canterbury and the people's favourite saint for nearly two centuries – Charles Dickens even name-drops him in *A Christmas Carol* – because it is purported he recovered from leprosy and avoided temptation from the Devil himself.

The Roman Catholic church was built in his honour in 1100, when London's population was little more than 15,000. St Paul's Cathedral had not been finished yet and most inhabitants still hired boatmen to row them across the river – it would be another 76 years before the first stone of London Bridge would be laid. The town's maze of lanes was lined by houses made of whitewashed lime or timber. The latter would spell disaster for this early version of the church, which was severely damaged by the Great Fire of London in 1666 which claimed 16,000 houses and 86 other churches.

St Dunstan in the East, one of London's little-known oases of calm.

ALSO TRY

Hidden Tube Stations, London, UK: Beneath some of the capital's busiest streets are forgotten and unused parts of the London Underground including Down Street, where Sir Winston Churchill sheltered during World War II. On certain days every year Transport for London opens them to the curious.

Sky Garden, London, UK: Inhale the oxygen of a garden located 160m (525ft) in the air. Situated at the top of a skyscraper nicknamed the Walkie Talkie, it offers cool clean air away from the smog of the city and photo-worthy aerial views of the capital.

Highgate Cemetery, London, UK: It may sound macabre, but there is something very peaceful about spending an afternoon around souls already at rest. This atmospheric leafy North London cemetery is the final resting place of several famous people, including philosopher Karl Marx, singer George Michael and author George Eliot, to name a few.

St Dunstan was patched up and treated to the addition of a Gothic-style steeple and tower by Sir Christopher Wren – the famed architect who had by now started work on St Paul's Cathedral – but disaster struck again during World War II when a bomb hit it in 1941. Only the north and south walls and Wren's steeple survived. After the war, it was decided St Dunstan would not be rebuilt, leaving it as one of the last remnants of the Blitz in the UK and an informal memorial to the city's resilience.

The ruins were eventually declared a public garden in 1970 and time has seen ivy and creeping flowers claim the rubbled arches while mature trees spring up in the courtyard.

City slickers that work in the surrounding area come at lunchtime to escape the air-conditioned hustle and bustle of the office and unwind for half an hour. Some read a book while munching their sandwich; others tilt their heads back and soak up the sun when it shows its face.

Sit and absorb the vibe of a structure that has stood in this spot – in one form or another – for almost a millennium and is now a bijou island of nature sandwiched between the glass-and-steel skyscrapers.

Escape the office on your lunchbreak and regroup amid the ancient walls of St Dunstan in the East, London.

Step back in time for art with a twist

THE MET CLOISTERS, NEW YORK, USA

It's possible to find peace in Manhattan if you know where to look

Manhattan is one of the noisiest places on Earth. A frenzy of yellow cabs honking their horns, the shrill juddering of jackhammers and the humming ambition of 1.7 million New Yorkers sardined onto an island 3.7-km (2.3-miles) wide and 21-km (13-miles) long. Finding a quiet moment in, perhaps, the most famous city in the world seems a big ask.

And yet, there is an oasis amid this skyscraper metropolis. Everyone's heard of The Met – short for The Metropolitan Museum of Art – where fashion magazine *Vogue* hosts the glitzy celebrity-studded Met Gala each year to raise funds for the museum, the largest of its kind in the USA – yet few people are aware of its little sister, The Met Cloisters, located in Fort Tryon Park on the northern tip of Manhattan, overlooking the Hudson River.

Something of an architectural marvel and the USA's only museum dedicated exclusively to the art of the Middle Ages, this modern building (constructed during the 1930s' Great Depression) incorporates sections of original French medieval monasteries.

Its conception started with George Grey Barnard, a student of the French sculptor Auguste Rodin. While studying in France, Barnard supplemented his earnings by selling medieval sculptures that he had procured from local landowners. He built up his own collection of art, too, and when he moved back to the USA, he opened a modest museum displaying it. A few years later, oil magnate John D Rockefeller bankrolled The Metropolitan Museum of Art so they could buy Barnard's collection to which Rockefeller donated 40 works of art from his own medieval collection, including a set of seven tapestries depicting – most unusually – the hunt of a unicorn. A larger space was needed, so the idea of The Met Cloisters was conceived.

The quiet corners of the Met Cloisters are the ideal escape from frenetic Manhattan, New York City.

THE LOWDOWN

How to do it: LaGuardia is the closest international airport to Manhattan. From there, you can catch a cab to The Met Cloisters or, if travelling by public transport, take the M60 bus from any terminal to 125th Street and then switch to the A subway and ride it to 190th Street. It's a ten-minute walk along Margaret Corbin Drive to The Met Cloisters, or you can hop on the M4 bus for one stop. Tickets can be purchased in advance online and offer entry to both Met locations. Open daily, except Wednesdays.

Best time of year: New York is always a good idea. However, summers can be extremely muggy – and smelly when the trash cans start to overflow. Best to enjoy it between April and June when The Met Cloisters gardens' trees are in bloom and the air fresh with the promise of spring.

ALSO TRY

Nikolaj Kunsthal, Copenhagen, Denmark: A much-respected contemporary art museum housed in the central St Nikolaj Church, whose blue-patina spire is easy to spot on Copenhagen's skyline. Its calming stark-white interior is the backdrop to ever-changing displays by Danish and international artists.

Kiscelli Museum, Budapest, Hungary: In the wooded part of Óbuda, the subdued yellow façade of this Baroque monastery, built in the 1800s, has a permanent collection detailing local history, but come for the cutting-edge art installations displayed in the cavernous dark moody interior of the ruined church.

Museo Luigi Bailo, Treviso, Italy: With bucketfuls of wow-factor, this fully restored 15th-century Renaissance monastery now serves as a contemporary art gallery, whose blend of sand-coloured stucco, Carrara marble and glass offers a serene minimalist space to escape the summer crowds of this popular northern Italian town.

A dynamic mix of modern architecture and old French monasteries, the Met Cloisters is the lesser-visited little sister of the Metropolitcan Museum of Art.

The chronological display of artworks, ranging from the 9th to the 15th centuries, includes paintings (look out for Robert Campin's *Annunciation Triptych*), tapestries, stained glass windows, statues and relics, including a miniature prayer book once owned by the Queen of France. But it's the vaulted ceilings and ornate columns of the monastery, castle, portal and church fragments – and all their details – that really wow visitors into silence.

Tread the same flagstones on which monks once stood in the Chapter House of Notre-Dame-de-Pontaut, a French abbey that was used as a farm – there's still an iron tether ring for horses pinned to one of the stone columns – before it was brought to the USA. Gaze up at the 12th-century Fuentidueña Apse, on loan from San Martin de Fuentidueña chapel in Spain, which was dismantled block by limestone block (3,300 of them) and sent via ship in 1958 to be reassembled in New York. It features a mural of the Virgin and Child and an arresting sculpture of Jesus on the Cross suspended in mid-air above the altar space.

Surrounding the gallery are three tranquil cloister gardens: some sown with wildflowers, another with culinary and medicinal herbs historically grown in medieval gardens, including those even used in magic spells. These sheltered spots are ideal for quiet contemplation, while the larger Fort Tryon Park, with its heather and alpine gardens, also offers views of George Washington Bridge. Immersed amid the greenery, its steel silhouette is a distant reminder that you're still on one of the busiest island on Earth.

Locate a green lung a stone's throw from an urban metropolis

YANGMINGSHAN NATIONAL PARK, TAIWAN

THE LOWDOWN

How to do it: Taoyuan International Airport serves Taipei. From the city centre take shuttle bus 260 which departs daily every 20 minutes from Shimin Boulevard behind Taipei Main Station. The journey to Yangmingshan takes about an hour. From there bus 108 loops around the park and can drop you at all the main attractions. Admission is free. Bring water, snacks and mosquito repellent, and wear a hat and sunscreen. Most travellers can visit Taiwan for 90 days without a visa.

Best time of year: The most popular time of year is late February and early March when the Yangmingshan Flower Festival celebrates the arrival of the cherry blossoms. From March to April the calla-lily fields bloom, and from October the autumn leaves create a canopy of orange. The only months to avoid are June, July and August, which are wet and humid.

This national park in Taiwan provides a vital green lung for the residents of Taipei and some wild nature for visitors

'Made in Taiwan' is a label plastered on everything from toys to electronics and with that comes the assumption that the entire island, located off the east coast of China, is one big industrial spread of skyscrapers and factories. But, in fact, Taiwan has nine national parks. One of them, Yangmingshan, in the far north, just 30 minutes from the neon-metropolis of Taipei, was named the world's first Urban Quiet Park by Quiet Parks International (see page 19).

The park is large – 114km² (44 sq miles), or the equivalent of 21,296 football pitches – and cannot be seen in a day, so you will have to single in on just a few sites. Its verdant hills, studded with lakes and waterfalls, are juxtaposed with dynamic valleys alive with steaming fumaroles and hot springs that gather around Mount Qixing, the highest (dormant) volcano in Taipei.

Also known as the Seven Star Mountain, this dormant peak's narrow moss-laced staircase offers a three-hour calf-tautening climb past seas of bamboo grass and (often) layers of rain-heavy cloud, to its 1,120-m (3,675-ft) summit. On a clear day, its crest rewards hikers with sweeping aerial views of Taipei. The descent leads you past cuts in the earth crusted with rotten-egg-smelling sulphur and the gas-belching Xiaoyoukeng fumarole.

Meanwhile, the park's other peak, Mount Datun, offers the best sunset views and between May and August the air around its slopes is filled with 168 species of butterflies. During the week, cars can trace a mountain road to the summit, but if you are visiting between October and February and the weather is clement, strap on your boots to tackle the five-hour Mount Datun Multi-Peak Trail. It involves a steep scramble through dense forest and an obstacle course of tree roots and rocks, including some roped sections (so bring gloves to protect your hands), but the raw nature is revitalizing – just be sure to keep an ear and eye out for snakes.

Visit between April and June to see a riot of hydrangeas in Taiwan's Yangmingshan National Park.

*Early risers are rewarded
with ethereal sunrises in
Yangmingshan National Park.*

A trail from Mount Datun's summit leads down to Erziping, a lake-studded clearing among the trees that is a prime spot for a picnic (avoid the weekend crowds) – alternatively, it is a manageable 30-minute walk along flat terrain from the main road. Another family friendly location is Qingtiangang, a spread of meadows where water buffaloes graze and can be watched from the safety of a broad well-maintained path with a guardrail. Its easy-to-reach-location makes it popular, so it is best to visit early in the morning, or later in the afternoon. A trail leading off from here takes you to the tannin-coloured waters of Lenshuikeng, a hot spring – that is really only lukewarm – where hikers like to soothe their soles after their walk. En route, take a detour to the modest-but-lush Juansi Falls, where jungle claws at the fast-flowing stream.

ALSO TRY

Hampstead Heath, London, UK: Beloved for its meadows, ancient woodland and natural swimming ponds, this iconic green space attracted all the Romantics – Keats, Shelley, Byron and Coleridge – and was declared Europe's First Urban Quiet Park on World Listening Day in 2021. Its sweeping views of London's skyline are most peaceful midweek.

Parc del Montnegre i el Corredor, Barcelona, Spain: Under an hour north of Barcelona, this designated Urban Quiet Park, filled with cork oaks and pine forests, offers green stillness amid one of the country's most densely populated regions.

Dender-Mark, Flanders, Belgium: Northern Belgium is one of the most urbanized areas in the world. This tranquil patch of nature sandwiched between the rivers Dender and Mark was recognized as Belgium's First Urban Quiet Park in 2021.

Parts of this national park do not feel wild at all – there are plenty of paths and buildings – but others feel positively Jurassic. What is certain, is that this is a vital green lung for the 2.6 million residents of Taipei and a breath of fresh air for travellers wanting to escape the city smog.

Spend a long weekend in the world's quietest city

ZURICH, SWITZERLAND

It is always worth looking beyond a city's acquired reputation and discovering the little-known peaceful joys it has to offer

Zurich's location is almost Disney-esque in its perfection. Just north of the Alps, it sits on the upper tip of the smiling Lake Zurich and stretches between two forested chains of hills with the oh-so-blue Limmat River coursing between them. Its *Altstadt* (old town) skyline is punctuated not by high-rises, but by a mix of Gothic, Renaissance, Romanesque and Baroque bell towers, church steeples and gabled façades daubed in candy colours.

These quaint streets have won it the accolade of least noise-polluted city in the world in a survey conducted by the World Hearing Index. But quiet does not equate with dull.

Zurich is often pegged as a strait-laced city inhabited solely by bankers and businesspeople, where the public transport runs as efficiently and accurately as the country's famous Swiss watches. The latter is true, but its spotless cobbled streets – James Joyce, who sought refuge here during World War I, once claimed Bahnhofstrasse (the main street) was so clean 'that one could drink minestrone soup off the pavement' – also brim with theatres, museums and art galleries. The city's quiet verve has enticed other great names over the years too, including physicist Albert Einstein and composer Richard Wagner, and it continues to attract a new generation of young creatives.

Instead of visiting modernist Marc Chagall's famed stained-glass windows in Fraumünster abbey, they seek out the Blüemlihalle, a crimson wash of flowery 1920s frescoes emblazoned across the vaulted-arch ceiling of the city police headquarters. They swap well-known hangouts such as the Odeon Café – where Einstein and Lenin ate their breakfast – for eclectic chill-out spaces such as Frau Gerolds Garten, built

Zurich's famous Fraumünster church reflected in the Limmat River at sunrise.

THE LOWDOWN

How to do it:
Switzerland's cultural hub can be reached easily by plane, rail and car. Zurich Airport is a 20-minute drive north of the city centre, which has one of the world's most efficient and reliable transportation networks. Trams, buses, trains and boats service all areas – and they are all included if you purchase a Swiss Travel Pass.

Best time of year:
The summer months between June and August are the most expensive and busiest, but also when the rivers and lakes are warm enough to swim in.

Vienna, Austria: This metropolis of palaces and courtyards is often billed as the second-most quiet city in the world. Stroll along the banks of the broad Danube, indulge in a steamy stress-busting thermal bath, kick back in cafés overlooking vineyards, and finish the day being serenaded by the world-famous Vienna Philharmonic orchestra.

Oslo, Norway: The country that invented the concept of *hygge* ('cosiness') excels at finding ways to celebrate it across the capital: from garden districts such as Ullevål Hageby and the coffee bars and traditional 19th-century wooden houses of Kampen to river swimming pools in Nydalen.

Munich, Germany: Unencumber yourself by shedding your swimsuit for a dip and steam inside the Art Nouveau Müller´sches Volksbad; sunbathe starkers in one of the city's six designated urban naked zones; or just hole up at Isarbräu – an 1890s railway station turned beer garden – for a steaming bowl of beer soup.

from shipping containers and featuring a vegetable garden and art gallery, or Rote Fabrik, an old factory used for poetry slams and concerts. They catch a boat to the peaceful island of Ufenau in Lake Zurich, site of a Roman settlement, medieval churches and an open-air art exhibition; or survey the stars from the Urania observatory, right in the heart of the city. And they seek out hushed green spaces such as the formal French-style gardens of Rechberg nestled between the university buildings, and the mythical creatures that roam Bruno Weber Park north of the centre.

For Zurich is a city that engages the senses. The snow-muffled silence of winter brings the taste of bubbling cheesy bowls of fondue or raclette and the sweet scent of *heisse schoggi* (artisanal hot chocolate) to defrost wind-cherried noses and frost-bitten hands; the sounds of Christmas stories being read to children by angels aboard the Märlitram; the swoosh of world-class skiing at the likes of Flumserberg and Sattel-Hochstuckli under one-and-a-half hour's drive away; the whoosh of wind on your cheeks as you toboggan down the slopes of Uetliberg; and the sensation of a steamy sauna at Seebad Enge followed by a plunge into the frigid waters of Lake Zurich. Meanwhile summer brings scoops of sweet *gelati*, hilly hikes amid wafts of wildflowers, and the cool splash of riverside baths and pools that, come nightfall, transform into open-air *Badi-Bars* alive with poetry readings and movie screenings.

So, if you are visiting as part of a long weekend, don't rush around trying to do it all. Seat yourself in a park for a few hours and watch local life unfold; delight in the muffled squeal that escapes your lips as the cool waters of the lake embrace you; and sit back and marvel at the fact that you can see the stars right in the heart of this misjudged city.

RIGHT *A snowy walk on the banks of Lake Zürich.*

OPPOSITE *Catch a ferry to the historic Isle of Ufenau on Lake Zürich.*

Listen to your body in one of the quietest places on Earth

ORFIELD LABORATORIES ANECHOIC CHAMBER, MINNEAPOLIS, USA

THE LOWDOWN

How to do it: Saint Paul International Airport is the gateway to Minneapolis. Orfield Labsoratories offers visits, which should be booked via email, Monday to Friday 9am–3pm starting at US $125 per person. For US $600 per hour, travellers wanting to see how long they can last can undertake The Orfield Challenge, where you have to stay in the chamber for an hour or longer to see if you can break the record. Afterwards, you'll be gifted a certificate of time achieved.

Best time of year: There's no ideal time to be locked in a sound-proof box! Just ensure you're mentally prepared for the challenge.

It's an experience you wouldn't forget, hearing the beating of your heart

Imagine the quietest place you've ever been. Conjure the feeling of being cocooned in utter peace – and yet, if you listen closely there would still be some noise. The hum of the heating, or a breeze murmuring through the curtains, the tick of a clock, or the distant chirrup of a bird. Life is always there, whispering in our ear.

But tucked away in a nondescript low-rise building in Minneapolis, is the Orfield Laboratories Anechoic Chamber – once the quietest place on Earth. Microsoft stole the record in 2015 with the creation of its own anechoic chamber, a record currently being contested.

Orfield's anechoic chamber, made of 1-m (3-ft) deep fibreglass wedges, insulated steel and concrete, absorbs 99.99 per cent of sound in the rated measurement range. It's used by the consumer, commercial and medical industries to develop products, such as perfecting the sound of an automotive switch or making quieter electric engines; it's used to research perceptual comfort in architecture for those with a hypersensitivity to noise, such as sufferers of post-traumatic stress disorder, and NASA uses a similar chamber to train their astronauts to adapt to the silence of space.

It is so silent that noise is measured in negative decibels. To give you a sense of scale, the peaceful bedroom you have in your mind's eye would probably register at 30dBA, your breath at 10dBA, but in the insulated chamber instruments can measure down to -13dBA for long periods of time, and greater than -22dBA for shorter periods – quieter than anything found in nature. The human ear stops registering sound at zero decibels, and when our ears receive no stimuli from the outside, they listen to the body. In here, *you* become the sound. The room is so quiet you can hear the *shhh* of blood coursing through your veins, the grinding of your bones and the *lub-dub* beat of your heart. You can speak, but there will be no echo.

The absence of sound can have odd effects. When walking or standing we use noise to orientate ourselves, but when we're deprived of those sensory cues, our sense of balance topples and, if you visit, you'll find yourself having to sit down.

Writer Bill Hanstock reports it being 'a bit trippy' and experiencing 'a sense of weightlessness, as though my consciousness was separating from my body...as though I was stretching in all directions and my being was filling the void.' Unsurprisingly, they say introverts fair better with the sensory deprivation than extroverts upon entering the womb-like space.

Guests normally have anything from a few minutes to a couple of hours inside the chamber, but to better understand the nature of pure silence, the head of the facility encourages people to stay longer and to steer clear of loud sounds and music immediately before the experience to avoid something called Temporary Threshold Shift, a reduction in hearing sensitivity, so when you pace across that mesh floor your ears are primed to listen inwardly. Welcome to the world's ultimate relaxation room.

In 2015, Orfield Laboratories lost its title in the Guinness World Records as the 'quietest place on Earth' to Building 87 inside Microsoft's headquarters in Redmond, Washington, USA. This 6m² (65 sq ft) cube, lined with spiky wedges of fibreglass foam, crowning six layers of concrete, clocks readings of -20.6dBA (compared to Orfield's -13dBA for long periods (their second Guinness World Record in 2013) and greater than -22dBA for short periods, like Microsoft). According to Microsoft engineer Hundraj Gopal: 'If a fighter plane took off just outside the room, you would barely hear it.' Unfortunately, it's not open to visitors.

The anechoic chamber at Orfield Laboratories – the second quietest place on Earth.

FUN FACT
Sound 80: Orfield Laboratory also houses Sound 80, the world's first digital recording studio, which has hosted artists such as Bob Dylan, Prince and Cat Stevens.

Follow the inspiration of artists

ARLES, FRANCE

THE LOWDOWN

How to do it: Marseille Provence Airport is the best serviced by international airlines. From there, it's a 50-minute drive to Arles (there are car rental companies at the airport), or you can take the airport shuttle to Marseille's Vitrolles railway station and catch the 1-hour direct train. Alternatively, Nîmes Alès Camargue Cévennes airport is only a 20-minute drive from Arles, but has fewer international routes. If you're travelling from Paris, direct trains depart regularly from Paris Gare de Lyon and take 7 hours.

Best time of year: Arles is at its liveliest between June and September when the *ferias* (festivals) take place, so for peace and quiet visit at the end of September/early October when the sun still has lingering warmth and the summer crowds have dissipated, or in spring before they arrive.

Arles, in the south of France, is a très jolie city that transports you back in time

With a double billing on the UNESCO World Heritage List, Arles comprises a clutch of biscuit-hued stone houses clustered around a (rare) intact 2,000-year-old Roman amphitheatre, modelled on the Colosseum in Rome. It boasts the most Roman remains in a city anywhere in the world after the Italian capital, including a theatre and baths. And yet, it receives relatively few visitors. Outside the summer months, you'll mostly have the streets of this ancient Gaul stronghold to yourself.

The city's second UNESCO award was granted because it sits on one of the four medieval pilgrimage routes crossing France towards the holy city of Santiago de Compostela in Spain, where the apostle St James is buried. Pilgrims pass through here and have their Camino Pilgrim passport stamped at the Alyscamps necropolis – one of the largest Christian cemeteries in the western world.

However, Arles also has a third winning attraction, noticed only by those who take the time to look deeply: the quality of the light – all soft russets, lemons and golds that set the stones aglow. Creatives who took notice include Paul Gauguin and Pablo Picasso – who used to watch bullfights inside the amphitheatre here. But one artist lingered longer and left a legacy...

In February 1888, a 35-year-old Vincent van Gogh wandered into Arles and, mesmerized by the honeyed rays, settled here for 16 months and produced a staggering 300 paintings and drawings. Follow in his footsteps on walking tours around town. Sip a coffee at Café La Nuit, subject of his *Café Terrace at Night* or stroll the Quai du Rhône, where he painted *Starry Night Over the Rhône*. Even the 16th-century hospital van Gogh visited after cutting off his ear still stands and now serves as the Espace van Gogh for exhibitions.

Arles has a rare intact Roman amphitheatre.

ALSO TRY

Lille, France: A stone's throw from the Belgian border and a Eurostar stopover, this former European Capital of Culture has the architecture and flair to rival Brussels but is blissfully quiet in comparison. A foodie heaven, you can spend long peaceful hours in time-worn cafés tucking into the likes of *carbonades flamandes.*

Ortygia, Sicily, Italy: Described by Roman philosopher Cicero 'as the greatest Greek city and the most beautiful of them all', Ortygia is the historical centre of Syracuse and accessed via a bridge. Get lost amid the ancient alleys and don't miss the daily outdoor market heaving with sumptuous Sicilian fare near the Temple of Apollo ruins.

Stockholm, Sweden: Surrounded by lake-dotted nature reserves, the Swedish capital has a rich mix of peaceful pockets: from the UNESCO-listed cemetery of Skogskyrkogården, to the medieval town of Sigtuna and the organic farm café of Rosenhill on the city fringes.

He painted his celebrated works *Bedroom in Arles* and *Chair* to decorate his rented rooms in the yellow house on Place Lamartine (before it was destroyed during World War II), in anticipation of a visit from Gauguin.

Fans of his ethereal and passionate brushstrokes can spend quiet hours at the Fondation Vincent van Gogh gallery, which puts on ever-changing exhibitions centering around his masterpieces. Art lovers will also enjoy the 150-year-old Musée Réattu, featuring several works by Picasso, and the ultra-modern steely LUMA for modern creations. Perhaps pick up a paintbrush of your own?

If the streets of the city feel too constrictive, the town also serves as the gateway to the Camargue – France's Wild West region where *gardians* (cowboys) still herd black bulls, flamingos flock to the salty dunes and groups of wild white horses canter across water-logged fields. Head for Salin de Giraud, a hamlet with absolutely nothing: no hotel, restaurant or grocery store for miles around, but famous for its *fleur de sel* saltpans, rich birdlife, and a 6-km (4-mile) long sandy beach that, for most of its length, allows naturism – making it the largest naturist beach in France. Strip off and feel the Mistral wind whistling across your bare bits. This raw region is steeped in history and legend that makes for a laidback city break with a real difference.

LEFT *It's as if an artist spilled their paints along Arles' picture-pretty streets.*

BELOW *Arles from above.*

Seek solitude among the dead

CAPUCHIN CRYPT, ROME, ITALY

THE LOWDOWN

How to do it: Rome–Fiumicino or Leonardo da Vinci is the main international airport. Transfers into the city can be arranged via taxi, bus or train. The bus is the cheapest and takes around 50 minutes, while the non-stop Leonardo Express train takes 30 minutes. The nearest metro stop for the Capuchin Crypt is Barberini on Line A. The crypt is open daily except holidays but tickets cannot be bought in advance. However, you can skip the queues by booking a 45-minute guided tour (available in English, Italian and Spanish) two weeks in advance through GetYourGuide or Tiqets. It's a religious site, so cover shoulders and knees.

Best time of year: Rome is at its busiest from May to September. So best to visit in April or October and November – it'll be quieter and you'll benefit from low-season prices.

Where to find silence in one of the most visited cities in the world? Go below

English poet Lord Byron declared Rome: 'the city of the soul!' And that it is. A high-drama, UNESCO-listed metropolis founded on a myth of murder – when Romulus killed his twin brother Remus and named the city after himself – and forged on a fission of high emotions: war and romance, gladiators and artists. Today, the lives of its close-to-three-million residents are played out against an ancient theatrical backdrop of ruins, gardens and cobbled streets.

But Rome doesn't stop at street level. Occupied for nearly 3,000 years, it descends layer upon layer back into the past. And in the throbbing heart, a little northeast of the coin-filled Trevi fountain, is Santa Maria della Concezione dei Cappuccini (Our Lady of the Conception of the Capuchins). This church sits on a macabre secret: a series of 500-year-old chapels lined with the bones and mummified remains of an estimated 4,000 individuals.

Pass through the museum (which features Caravaggio's *St Francis in Meditation* among its artefacts), descend into a corridor dimly lit by (electric) candles and come face-to-face with death. This is art as you've never seen it. Thousands upon thousands of human bones – scapulas, spines, ribs, fibulas and femurs – artistically arranged in elaborate patterns on the walls and ceilings of five of the six crypts.

At the centre of a skull-framed altar hang two severed mummified arms crossed to form the Capuchin coat of arms. Elsewhere bones have been crafted into chandeliers; while in other rooms robed and hooded figures leer over visitors, their skulls still papered with desiccated skin.

There's little in the main church of Our Lady of the Conception of the Capuchins that gives away the dark secret that lies beneath her.

The crypts are believed to house the remains of some 4,000 souls.

ALSO TRY

Père Lachaise, Paris, France: The final resting place of Jim Morrison (lead singer of The Doors) and singer Edith Piaf (of *La Vie en Rose* fame) to name a few. The French capital's largest cemetery is the most-visited necropolis in the world, but it doesn't feel like it on an autumnal day when the low sun lights up the russet leaves and you can stroll the famous graves alone.

Ani, Kars, Turkey: Snuggled right up against the Armenian border in eastern Turkey, this little-visited UNESCO-listed Silk Road city was one of the world's largest cities until it was sacked by the Mongols in 1236. Today, its crumbling collection of Gothic churches with exquisite hand-painted murals sit amid grassy plains in the middle of nowhere.

Nubian royal pyramids, El-Kurru, Sudan: The Black Pharaohs ruled Egypt for over a century during the 25th Dynasty and several of their royal family members were buried at El-Kurru – a hardly-heard-of archaeological site in northern Sudan. The tomb of Nubian King Tanutamun (not to be confused with Tutankhamun) is the most impressive of all.

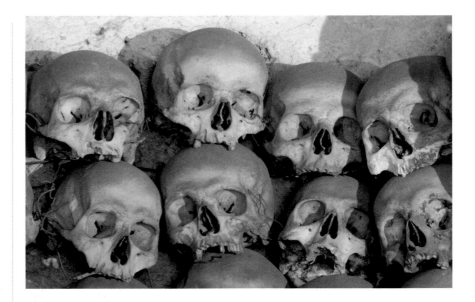

Why are they here? It's the legacy of the Capuchins, a Roman Catholic branch of the Franciscan Friars established in 1525 by Matteo da Bascio who felt the order had drifted away from the authentic austerity advocated by St Francis of Assisi. Bascio swapped his habit for a brown hooded tunic called the cappuccino (from which the coffee takes its name), grew his beard, often went barefoot and took vows of poverty and solitude. The reformist movement faced many criticisms and wasn't recognized officially until 1619. Soon after, Pope Urban VIII – whose brother Antonio Barberini was, uncoincidentally, both a Capuchin *and* a Cardinal – dedicated funds to the construction of the chapels. Barberini had the remains of thousands of Capuchins excavated from Via dei Lucchesi Monastery and the bones displayed with grotesque artistry – a tradition that continued every time a brother died until 1870 when the burial of human remains within the city walls was criminalized.

Word of the shocking, yet awe inspiring, spectacle spread and was written about for the first time by the notorious French libertine, the Marquis de Sade. Today, the ossuary is a popular attraction, but the sight of the skulls plunges visitors into either a respectful silence or muted marvel, so there's little to disturb your silent experience.

For the Capuchins, this was far from a gory stunt, but rather a space to reflect on our own mortality. Written in the last chapel is the message: '*Quello che voi siete noi eravamo, quello che noi siamo voi sarete*,' meaning: 'Exactly what you are now we once were, and what we are now you will become.' A reminder that our last destination is always silence.

ABOVE *Look past the eerie and unearth the chance for silent reflection.*
OPPOSITE *Our Lady of the Conception of the Capuchins' cemetery.*

Reflect on the human cost of war

IN FLANDERS FIELDS MUSEUM, YPRES, BELGIUM

THE LOWDOWN

How to do it: Brussels Zaventem Airport is the international gateway to Belgium. Trains to Ypres, via Ghent, regularly depart from the airport. Car rental companies are on site and driving takes about an hour and a half. In Flanders Fields Museum is open daily from 10am to 5pm (6pm April–November).

Best time of year: Visiting during the commemoration of Armistice (11 November) is moving, but you'll need to book accommodation well in advance and the city is far busier. Also avoid the second Sunday of May, when the city celebrates its raucous Kattenstoet (Cat Parade).

Silence is a time-honoured way in which we show our respect to others

This award-winning, state-of-the-art World War I museum in Ypres, western Belgium, may not – as the chapter is entitled – be an 'urban oasis' in the traditional sense, but it's included in this book because certain sites deserve our silence. They stand as a reminder of past errors and ask us to reflect upon our sense of humanity.

Ypres – or 'Wipers' as it was nicknamed by British soldiers – is an ancient town that was caught in the very centre of Germany's Schlieffen Plan that aimed to sweep across Belgium and into France to occupy Paris and capture the seaports. German forces surrounded the city on three sides and bombarded it with relentless artillery fire, flattening the town and surrounding countryside until it was virtually unrecognizable and reducing the (now rebuilt) 13th-century Cloth Hall – in which the museum now stands – to its bare bones. The town was embroiled in not one, not two, but three battles as the Allies and Germans fought for, and lost, a stretch of high ground to the east. In these wars of attrition, both a young, and as yet unknown, Adolf Hitler and Winston Churchill fought on the front line.

The conflict claimed an estimated 600,000 lives and the In Flanders Fields Museum aims to conserve this link with the past to ensure we never forget the soldiers' sacrifice. Indeed, it may have been over a century since the war ended, but the landscape still bears traces: from excavated trenches to the trees which, when cut through, bear the blackened marks of bullets. The museum displays one: a slice of a 200-year-old oak felled in the 1990s whose inner rings are scarred by artillery fire.

Poppy wreaths laid in honour of World War I soldiers at the Menin Gate, Ypres, Belgium.

PREVIOUS *The In Flanders' Field Museum is housed in Ypres' Cloth Hall, which was almost completely flattened by artillery fire during World War I and then meticulously reconstructed between 1933 and 1967.*

ABOVE *La Belle Alliance Cemetery on the outskirts of Ypres is dedicated to British soliders who fought and died during the Great War.*

OPPOSITE *The personal belongings and uniforms of soldiers are among the most touching parts of the In Flanders' Field Museum, Ypres.*

The museum's aim is to bring a sense of scale to the unimaginable loss of life and it achieves this by asking visitors to input their name and place of birth into a computer on arrival and then sharing personal stories of people from your town or region who participated in the war. Mixed in with the interactive maps, films, uniforms and propaganda posters are glass cabinets displaying personal mementoes – pipes, family photos and identity papers – of individual men who fell during the fighting. Discreet hollowed-out columns, which adults can stand inside, also conceal black-and-white photographs taken by reporters of the horrific injuries sustained. It all combines to highlight the futility of war and reduce visitors to humbled muteness.

ALSO TRY

Genocide Memorial, Kigali, Rwanda: The final resting place for more than 250,000 (of an estimated 800,000) Tutsi victims killed during the 1994 Rwandan Genocide. The visitor centre aims to educate visitors about how such an atrocity came to pass and examines genocide in other countries. The memorial gardens are also a place for quiet contemplation.

Chernobyl National Museum, Kiev, Ukraine: Chernobyl Nuclear Power Plant overheated and exploded with the force of 500 nuclear bombs. This sobering museum details the events. Notice the video footage – filmed in Pripyat hours after the explosion – where the screen is flickering with static caused by the radiation and the locals are completely unaware of its effects.

Cambodia Landmine Museum, Siem Reap, Cambodia: Cambodia is still riddled with between four and six million land mines planted during the Khmer Rouge regime, with one out of every 300 Cambodians falling victim to one. This museum details that dark legacy and advocates the work of Aki Ra, a former child solider who went on to found Cambodia Self Help Demining (CSHD), a land-mine clearing organization and relief centre for affected children.

A small extra fee grants access to the belfry, a belltower located at the top of a steep spiral staircase that looks out over Menin Gate, whose walls are inscribed with the names of 54,896 British and Commonwealth soldiers whose graves are unknown, and beyond that, the uniform rows of white graves at Tyne Cot, the world's largest Commonwealth war-grave cemetery and the final resting place for 11,954 souls.

Warfare may not seem like an appropriate topic for children, but the museum aims to explain the war in a palatable manner by introducing them to Andrew, a 12-year-old boy born in Ypres, whose scrapbook introduces people and stories in the museum. An important move 'Lest we Forget'.

Find the quieter side of a city break to Germany

LEIPZIG, GERMANY

Perhaps it's the old buildings at the heart of Leipzig that give the city its peaceful feel

Most travellers have heard of boisterous Berlin, port-life Hamburg and Munich's beer-fuelled Oktoberfest, but little Leipzig, in eastern Germany, often flies under the radar. The 'Hero City' that quietly started the Peaceful Revolution (see page 241), is a music-and-arts town with no fewer than 19 museums amid a population of just over half a million and was the home of choice to composer heavyweights Johann Sebastian Bach, Felix Mendelssohn and Robert Schumann.

While other German cities replaced their World War II-damaged historic buildings with modern constructions, Leipzig initially couldn't afford to, so it left the Renaissance and Baroque merchant houses, city hall and churches as they were. When money did arise, they chose to repair instead of replace and, consequently, the old city is a preserved architectural gem and arguably Germany's prettiest city centre.

Begin your wanderings beneath the divine candy-pink and mint-green vaulted ceiling of St Nicholas Church, where Bach premiered many of his compositions, including the *St John Passion*, and site of the famous Monday Demonstrations (see box page 241).

Nearby is St Thomas, a white-washed Gothic church with a highly illustrious history. Martin Luther, the medieval priest who controversially married a former nun and was a key figure in the Protestant Reformation, preached here. An infant Richard Wagner was baptized here well before he lit up the world of opera. Wolfgang Amadeus Mozart played the organ here during his 1789 European tour and, best of all, this is the church where Bach served as cantor until his death in 1750. Pay your respects at his bronze-plated tomb. Fans of his work should cross the road to visit the Bach-Archive, which houses his instruments and hand-written sheet music.

Leipzig city centre at sunset.

SEYCHELLES

No visa required.

La Digue *seychelles.com/app-listing-details?ProductId=5fc5 e2a47d35d21730f781d3*

North Island *north-island.com*

Praslin *seychelles.com/app-listing-details?ProductId=5fc5e0 ba7d35d21730f781c9*

Silhouette Island *seychelles.com/app-listing-details?Product Id=5fc08a40f9e417167178dfe8*

SOUTH AFRICA

Visas are not required for stays of 90 days or less.

Dhamma Patākā *pataka.dhamma.africa*

SPAIN

Kausay *kausaycommunity.com*

Parc del Montnegre i el Corredor *quietparks.org/parc-del-montnegre-i-el-corredor-spains-first-urban-quiet-park*

ST HELENA

Ascension *ascension.gov.ac*

St Helena *sthelenatourism.com*

Tristan da Cunha *tristandc.com*

SUDAN

Visas are required and should be arranged prior to travel *sudan-embassy.co.uk*

Nubian royal pyramids *nationalgeographic.co.uk/travel/2017/07/sudan-africas-other-pyramids*

SWEDEN

Skinnskatteberg, Shambala Gatherings *shambalagatherings.com*

Stockholm *visitstockholm.com*

South Koster Island *vastsverige.com/en/stromstad/koster*

SWITZERLAND

Alpina Gstaad *thealpinagstaad.ch/en*

Zurich *zuerich.com/en*

Törbel, Kailash International Retreat Centre *kailash.org*

TAIWAN

Visas are not required for stays of 90 days or less.

Yangmingshan National Park *ymsnp.gov.tw/main_en/*

THAILAND

Dark Retreat Center *www.darkretreat.center*

TURKEY

Ani, Kars *nationalgeographic.co.uk/travel/2016/10/turkey-ancient-site-ani*

UKRAINE

Chernobyl National Museum *chornobylmuseum.kiev.ua/en*

Carpathian Mountains *green-ukraine.com/tourist-attractions-of-the-carpathian-mountains*

USA

ESTA or visa required for entry *travel.state.gov/content/travel/en/us-visas*

Alaska, Inside Passage *travelalaska.com/Destinations/Regions/Inside-Passage*

Alaska, Still Point Lodge *stillpointlodge.com*

California, Esalen Institute *esalen.org*

California, Redwood National and State Parks *nps.gov/redw/index.htm*

Colorado, Dunton Hot Springs *duntondestinations.com/hot-springs*

Haleakalā National Park *gohawaii.com/islands/maui/regions/upcountry-maui/haleakalā-national-park*

nps.gov/hale/index.htm

Hawaii, Vipassana Hawaii *vipassanahawaii.org*

Louisiana, Bayou Bartholomew *louisianatravel.com/paddle/trail/bayou-bartholomew-paddling-trail*

New York, Met Cloisters *metmuseum.org/visit/plan-your-visit/met-cloisters*

Minneapolis, Orfield Laboratories *orfieldlabs.com*

Montana, American Prairie Reserve *americanprairie.org*

WALES

Bardsey Island *bardsey.org/about*

ZAMBIA

Visas are required and can be purchased online *zambiahc.org.uk*

South Luangwa National Park, Art Safari *artsafari.co.uk*

INDEX

Page numbers in *italics* refer to illustrations

ACKNOWLEDGEMENTS

The publishers would like to thank the following for supplying images.

Taku Bannai for the beautiful illustrations.

All photos © Shutterstock.com with the exception of those listed below:

© Alamy.com, pg. 21, 30, 52, 60, 76, 82, 89, 90, 112, 146, 172, 173, 182, 191, 192, 211, 227, 228, 230, 234, 235, 237, 241, 242; ©Arteles/Teemu Räsänen, pg. 152, 154, 155; © Bali Silent Retreat, pg. 185; © Deborah Hanekamp, pg. 198; © Derek Galon/Getty Images, pg.47; © Emma Thomson, pg. 50, 68, 84, 124, 125, 139; © Hurtigruten/Dan Avila, pg. 64; © Mandali Retreat Center, pg. 201; © Mark Russell, pg. 72; © Plum Village Community of Engaged Buddhism, pg. 186, pg.189; © Redzaal/Getty Images, pg. 32-33; © Roman Khomlyak/Getty Images, pg.18; © Steve Horsfield, pg. 91; © Steve Orfield, pg. 221; © Stillpoint Lodge, pg. 165, pg. 166; © The Alpina Gstaad, pg. 178-181; © The Hermitage, pg. 175-177; © The Sharpham Trust, pg. 174; © Wild View Retreat, pg. 167-169.